EVERY MUM IS A SUPER MUM

Breaking Free From Overwhelm And Exhaustion

GW00400453

By Dr. 'Dunı

Warm Wishes

Dr Dunn

CONTENTS

DEDICATION

This book is dedicated to my Eternal God and Father who gave me my entire being- body, soul, mind and spirit and called me to live my purpose in spite of adversity.

To my father, Ayodele Adeniyi, the eminent man whose life gave me life and whose death gave me purpose. I honour you and celebrate you every day.

To my mum, Josephine, a woman of substance who is my supermum. I cannot thank you enough.

To my beautiful children, Kiitan & Jola, I am so privileged to be your mother.

ABOUT THE BOOK

This book is meant for all the supermums in the world. It is for all those amazing mothers who are doing everything that they can, who are struggling, who are suffering, who are feeling overwhelmed and exhausted. It is for those mothers who are feeling unworthy, guilty, or feeling like failures.

This book is to show mothers they do not have to go above and beyond to be supermums. Because every mum is a supermum not because of the super things that she does, but because of the superpowers she possesses within.

I am Dr. 'Dunni from Druwa Academy and my mission is to empower mums to recognise their superpowers, which they have always had, and break free from overwhelm and exhaustion while ensuring overall wellbeing.

I will discuss what to do when you are faced with these overwhelming situations. How to generate energy on a consistent basis, and knowing that it is okay for you to experience overwhelm and feel exhausted sometimes.

The ability to turn any situation around lies in your heart, in your hands and in your superpowers. When a mother's health is great, the whole household enjoys great health. When the mother's health is not great, the whole household suffers from ill health. Mother's health is so important because the mother does not only care for herself, but she cares for the younger generation.

The children who watch us as mothers would recognise the ways by which they can enhance their well-being on a consistent basis.

To benefit from this book, it is important to recognise how learning vary, how experiences vary and how you can learn from different sources and perspectives and become the better for it.

It requires that you have an open mind. It is not a prescription. It is not a get well fast scheme. And it is not a condemnation of any population or demographic. It is a tool of empowerment for every mum living and every mum coming after, to see and know they are supermums.

This book is not for you if you resent the idea of having superpowers, or the idea of mums being empowered, unleashed, unlimited and flourishing,

INTRODUCTION

Getting rid of overwhelm and exhaustion is an important topic, especially for mums. Over the years, we have seen increased stress experienced by mums.

With the evolution from the era of women being predominantly housewives to the modern era where most households need both partners working to support the household, we have an increasing number of mums needing to have a 9-5 job or even a part-time job.

They are still required to take care of the family, tidy and clean up the house, take care of business, run side hustles and also ensure they are the personal assistance of their partners, their children, and all who require such services.

Acknowledging that there are differences in culture and expectations placed on mums, some mums are also laden with the responsibility of maintaining the relationship between the extended family and their own nuclear family.

The expectations and the pressure on mothers is immense. Society has made that so. Many cultures emphasise the need of mothers to ensure the house is clean, the children are fed and cared for, the husband is well taken care of and is satisfied with every aspect of life, and that tasks are done according to the expectations of others with no concern for her welfare.

In addition, she must find time to bring income into the family, do the bookkeeping, ensure she is available for events in the family, or in the community and be the powerhouse.

We all know that these expectations are tall orders and quite demanding. In some cases, she might do them, and itmay seem effortless.

However, while she appears to be gliding on the pond, you do not notice that her legs are kicking beneath the surface at a 1000miles/hr. Unfortunately, this takes a toll on her well-being.

Unless the mother in this scenario is able to recognise how she feels and nurture her spirit, soul, mind and body she will be drained, exhausted, overwhelmed and eventually burnout.

For this reason, we are recognising and addressing these issues before they become a problem. If however, it has already become a problem and resulted in several losses, There is still something that can be done.

Remember, whatever you have experienced would serve as a foundation to a more emotionally resilient you. Whatever difficulties that come your way can be surmounted.

If you are going through that situation, because you can't go around it, going through it, is only going to make you stronger and better.

So for those mums out there who are under the duvet crying, feeling ashamed, guilty and drained or listening to the criticism of others, I am here to tell you that you are a super mum and no one can take that away from you.

Later in this book, we are going to explore ways by which you, as a mum can take care of the people you care for while ensuring you are optimising your well being physically, emotionally, mentally, socially, financially, so you can live the life of abundance you desire and deserve. I will address this from my own experience, my knowledge, the knowledge and experience of others and my ability to recognise and interpret scenarios.

At this point, I would like to mention that this is for information. It is not a medical advice column, or book and it is not specific to your situation. So if you need any professional help, support or input, do get in touch with your trained professional, who has access to your records, and is able to make an informed decision on your care with your involvement in the consultation.

If any of these stories is triggering for you, please reach out to someone who can support you, and help you through the process.

The aim of this book is to ensure that you, as a mum, recognise and see important changes you can make on a consistent basis to enhance your wellbeing. It is not a quick fix. And it is also not a get rich quick scheme. It is all about improving your well-being consistently using practices, strategies and tools provided.

Mums, are you ready to see how you are able to break free from feeling overwhelmed and exhausted, care for yourself consistently and ensure your overall well-being?

CHAPTER ONE

I was lying in bed under the duvet. It was a Saturday morning and it was bright outside. I felt cold even though the heating was on. At one point, my daughter came over to me, 'Mummy, Mummy,' she said, 'Let's go outside.' I looked at her and smiled. My darling I thought. She went on saying, 'Mummy, it snowed, let's go and play outside.'

Yes, overnight, it snowed. The children love to play in the snow, making snow angels, making a snowman and having snowball fights. While she was saying that her little brother was toddling around, grabbing the coats, getting ready to go out. At that point, I reached out and said, 'My darling, please come into bed and cuddle with mummy.'

She climbed into bed, and so did her little brother. And as they came in, I hugged them close. Here I was holding my beautiful children. I had told them to come into bed to cuddle with mummy AGAIN. This was not the first time but I did not have a choice.

I felt exhausted. I felt overwhelmed. I had recently lost my father and I was grieving. I was a shadow of myself. At that point, I had lost three dress sizes, was frightened all the time, and lacking energy. I felt like a failure as a mother. I couldn't even play with my children. I was holding them back from going outside to play like they wanted to.

I loved to play, but I just did not have the energy. So under the duvet, holding my children tears started to stream down my face. 'This had to stop,' I thought to myself.' I had to find a way. This could not continue. My children could not be impacted by this unfortunate circumstance.'

Without knowing what to do, where to turn, where to go, I made a decision that day. I was going to find answers. I was going to find means by which I could get out of this state of feeling overwhelmed and exhausted.

I read many books, listened to podcasts, did courses, and got coaches while seeking the answers. I did my study time at night when the children were asleep and I was not on call.

At that time, I was working full time as a doctor while also caring for my children. I knew I needed to find a way. Many strategies I learned did not apply to me. Some did, and I was able to put them into practice, while some I had to modify.

With trial and error and years of implementation, I was able to build my toolkit and uncover the framework that utilised my superpowers to ensure high energy level and improved well-being despite the many roles that I occupy on a daily basis.

On a particular day, when I was the medical oncall doctor, I got called to the ward at 3am. As I got there, I said, 'What's up people?' with so much excitement. People could not believe that I had so much energy at that time of the night. I could see myself transform from a state of overwhelm and exhaustion to having energy to do things I wanted to do, even at those very ungodly hours. I was able to work, have better focus, make better decisions and have greater productivity.

Most importantly, I was able to play with my children and enjoy their company. I watch them grow, learn what their strengths were, and empower them in those strengths. I still do so even today.

The practices did not lead me to spend hours toiling in the gym, or doing things that drained me, but they were simple practices that I could incorporate into my days that were packed with activities.

I am going to show you how I went through this and was able to build my clinical career, academic career, businesses, and actually impact the lives of people, nationally, and internationally in my roles as a life and well-being coach, family doctor, teacher, speaker, entrepreneur and mum. I will show what this process has been and how you can consistently break free from overwhelm and exhaustion even on those challenging days.,

I am an eternal student. And I am constantly learning new things. I do not believe this is the end of the journey for me. I learn new ways of enhancing my well-being, of ensuring that I can live that life of abundance I desire and deserve. I am sure that while I am doing this, I am showing my children how to be, how to live and helping them to make those choices that will bring about their ultimate goals and their ultimate purpose for being here on Earth.

While I am a medical doctor, some of the things I will be sharing might have some basis in science that I learned in medical school, or even in elementary and high school. However, most of it was done by self-learning, personal development and applying those principles to the science and the art of living holistically well.

As I continue to grow, I will continue to share. As I continue to grow, I will continue to be present for you. As I continue to grow, I will continue to show you what is possible and available to you. Of course, things may change, principles may vary, but at this point they are working, they are learnable, and they are doable.

As I perform my many roles, I recognise there are times when I have a lot to do. These are moments where I could naturally feel overwhelmed. However, I pay close attention to the language I use, the importance of recognising my entire being- who I am, who I am becoming and my purpose in life.

These are some of the things that helped me move from a state of overwhelm, and in some cases prevented me from getting to that stage at all. The ability to get rid of frustration, and move my energy from zero or negative to fullness enables me to achieve more. I am able to feel energetic in myself, do things that make me feel happy in the moment and experience joy.

So as I write this book, on this beautiful morning, I feel energised as I pour out my heart to you. I wish that this touches the life of a mum out there so she can know that all things are possible. You have got the superpowers within you that you just need to tap into. And as you tap into those superpowers, more will unfold to you because it is infinite.

So, what do you say? Do you want to come on this journey with me? Do you want to see how you can use your knowledge of being a human being, of being a woman, of being alive, of having the knowledge of your body, your mind, your soul, and spirit to enhance your wellbeing?

CHAPTER 2- PERSPECTIVE IS EVERYTHING

Have you ever wondered why something bad happened? That question came to the forefront of my mind repeatedly when my father died. However, I soon realised that while it was a painful experience, grieving the loss of my father that was the moment that brought me down this journey of self-discovery and personal development.

If my father had not died, if I was not grieving, if I did not feel like a failure as a mother, if I did not go through this tragedy, the difficult moments and the circumstances that surrounded my losses, I probably will not be on this journey. I would definitely not know as much as I know now. I would not have had the experiences that I have now.

So I say thank you for the pain, the losses and the circumstances, painful though they were. As I make this statement, I recall the lyrics of the song by ABBA- 'so I say thank you for the music, the song I am singing...' I digress, but as I do, a smile comes to my face and a jig comes to my hips.

It is said that knowledge is power. I however would state that Knowledge is potential power. It only becomes power when it is applied. This then becomes a way of being when it is practised consistently. Not only would it bring about the goals and outcomes that we desire but it would draw us closer to our purpose.

This purpose became apparent to me as I experienced a deepening spiritual connection which saw me through this journey. As I applied what I was learning, I was sharing my knowledge and experience with those around me. I remembered that while I was sharing this with people I encountered on a daily basis, I still felt terrified of going out there, and sharing it with the rest of the world.

This continued until one day while I was having my morning devotion, which I do daily. I was reading from the scriptures, the Gospel of Matthew. And there was a beautiful story that I had read many times before.

It was the story of the king, who had three servants. He was going on a journey to a faraway land and he decided to entrust these three servants with talents according to their ability. To the first servant, he gave five talents, the second he gave two talents, and the third, he gave one talent. And off he went.

After some time, he returned, and upon his return, the first servant came to him and said, 'Oh, King, I am glad you are back. You gave me five talents. I went and traded and I got five more. Here are 10 talents.' The king was pleased and commended him, calling him a good and faithful servant. He said, 'you have been faithful in little things, I will trust you with more.'

The second servant then came in to give account to the king. He said, 'You gave me two talents. I went and traded. And I got two more. So here we have four talents.' And the king again commended this servant, referring to him as a good and faithful servant. 'You have been faithful in little things,' he said. 'I will entrust you with more.'

Then the third servant comes in and says, 'Oh King, I am glad you're back. You gave me one talent. I was afraid so I hid it.'

When I read that part of Scripture, I started to weep. I was crying because I knew that at that point, even though I had read the story many times before that was me. I was that servant, who had been given a talent.

But because I was afraid, I hid it. I may have expressed the talents, wisdom, knowledge, and experience, to my clients, patients, relatives, friends and to the people I came into contact with, but that was not my purpose. My purpose was to help people globally.

At that point, I made the decision not to hide anymore. I decided to work through that fear of the unknown, fear of criticism, fear of rejection and place my trust in God who had given me this talent to do, according to my ability what I know I can do. Here I am today based on that decision that was made on that day, sharing with you what I have learnt. That talent I was given would be used to empower mums globally to step into their superpowers, because they can and because of who they are, and whose they are. This has been an inspiration for me.

REFLECTION

When you are faced with a difficult situation, a painful situation or an obstacle in your path,

1. how do you view it?
2. Do you view it as the end?
3. Do you view it as a potential for upliftment?
4. When you are overwhelmed, how do you handle it?
5. What has been your turning point?
6. What triggered that turning point?
7. What enabled you to move from that state? (if you have moved from that state)

In my case, I had decisions made in the moment. After making those decisions, I took action. Take action today. Throughout the book, you will have some questions for reflection. Use a journal to capture your thoughts and insights. There will also be some suggested practices as you go along.

CHAPTER 3- WHY AVA FEELS THIS WAY

'You are useless. You are a failure. How could you do this? And you call yourself a mother.' These were the thoughts that were going round in Ava's mind as she lay on the floor, crying not knowing what to do. She was always feeling tired, struggling to pay her bills. She was frustrated. 'She could only do this now', she thought as she had dropped the children off at school.

But there was no energy and she still had to walk back home. She felt like she was losing her mind. She couldn't even look at herself in the mirror in the morning because she had so much pain within. She felt lonely. 'No one would talk to me, ' she said, 'I am useless.' She couldn't even think about meeting up with friends or seeking help from family. They were not close by.

So as she laid on the floor, crying, she could feel her heart pounding in her chest. She started to have some pain and tightness in her chest. She thought she was having a heart attack. 'Is this how I am going to die?', she thought. Then the evil thought came again. 'Well, you're better off dead. At least the children would not suffer.'

She cried even more wanting to scream, but she could not make a sound. She felt so much pain and could not even think about calling for help. She was breathing so fast and could hardly catch her breath. Terrified, she didn't know what to do. At that point, the letter popped through the post. It fell just a couple of feet away from where she laid. That distracted her.

'Oh,' she said, 'that is another bill. How am I going to pay that?' She didn't want to check. She didn't want to get off the floor. But she knew she needed to. There were so many things she needed to get sorted before it was time to pick up the children from school. More so, she could not continue this way.

Ava had been a single mother for a few years following a very unhappy and abusive marriage. The day she decided she was leaving, she had multiple thoughts questioning whether this was the right decision. With her background, and upbringing many shunned and criticised her and so she fell out with family and friends and did not seek any sympathy from either.

Because of the busyness of her day, she found it difficult to make new friends. Her social life was non-existent. Her children had classmates who laughed at them because they were from a broken home. Many times she had tried to help her children feel confident that she was there being everything to them, but she felt lost. She forgot who she was.

That is one thing many mums we do. We forget who we are.

There are so many Avas out there who are struggling. Many times our thoughts bring us down, telling us those negative disabling declarations of how useless we are, what a failure we are, and how no one cares, or wishes we were here. These causes overwhelm and sometimes it goes on to having thoughts to end one's life.

At those critical moments, some mothers have eventually done it. Some had, unfortunately, been successful, and others have not. It; however, does not have to be this way. Some mums like Ava, have been through situations whereby they struggle. They have chest pain; their heart is beating so fast. They feel like they are going to die. They feel like they are having a heart attack.

But then they do not know what to do in the moment. Not only do they have racing and worrying thoughts, they find themselves forgetful, quite disorganised, and struggling to concentrate, or even make decisions. Sometimes they make wrong choices. And after making the choices, they criticise themselves for the choices made. In some cases, they also get external criticism.

The constant thoughts that tell them that they are not worthy affect the way they feel causing them to feel upset, sad, depressed and in some cases, suicidal. Not only that, they have the emotional overwhelm of guilt, fear, anger, impatience, which could manifest as being more irritable, moody, struggling to connect with people, including the people around them.

Whenever they become irritable, and snap, unfortunately, they feel worse and isolate themselves further. When these emotional and mental causes impact our wellbeing it manifests physically in our bodies. Sometimes it comes as having low energy and feeling tired all the time. The worry also affects our sleep so that we have poor quantity and quality sleep. When we wake up, we do not feel rested.

As a result, we can have headaches, body aches and pains and tense muscles. This impacts our immune system, making us more at risk of developing infections. Sometimes even our gut, which has a mind of its own, decides to play up as well. So you have someone feeling bloated, having diarrhoea and/or constipation.

When this happens, the chemicals in your body, your hormones start to be produced in a way that reflects what you are going through. This vicious cycle affects their mental, emotional and physical well-being. We then succumb to overwhelm and exhaustion.

So I'm going to say it again. **'Every mum is a supermum not because of the super things that she does. But because of the superpowers she possesses within.'**

You may be going through what Ava was going through. You might feel alone, unheard or unappreciated.

I know what that feels like because I've been there. The ability to get out of this overwhelm, and exhaustion that we feel as mums require us to make a decision in that moment.

I've heard people in difficult situations; scream out, 'MAKE THIS STOP.' And that's exactly what many mums are screaming out. 'Make this stop. I want this to end.'

Making that decision is so important. It uncovers who you are when your mind is suggesting those disabling thoughts. When your mind is telling you what you can or cannot do, that is the moment when you speak up about who you are.

It is difficult, believe me, I know. It is even worse when you have been faced with self-doubt for a while because you feel unable to counteract those thoughts, or even go back to those glorious days where you remembered who you are.

Well, it's not too late. It is time. If you are Ava on the floor, or under the duvet, crying; if you are Ava in pain, in turmoil, feeling overwhelmed; if you are Ava, procrastinating, being forgetful, feeling lonely; I have news for you.

The ability to take yourself from that state of fear, anguish and pain lies within you. And I will show you how.

There are three reasons why every mum needs to get started in this process of breaking free from overwhelm.

1. You need to do it for you because you are worthy
2. You need to do it for you because you are awesome.
3. You need to do it for you because you are more than enough

You might be wondering why I repeated 'do it for you.' I did that three times because repetition helps you to remember concepts, it ingrains what you learn. That is the reason why when we were in elementary school; we said or sang the alphabet repeatedly from A to Z.

Many times we as mums put the needs of everyone before ours. We say to ourselves, 'I need to do this for my children. I need to do this for my partner. I need to do this for society. I need to do this for my church.' When we do that, either based on the expectations they have put on us or the expectations we have put on ourselves, we are faced with moments of pain, we are setting ourselves up for exhaustion and overwhelm.

However, when you are rightly placed at the centre, the result is phenomenal. What stops most mums from stepping up into the decision to break free from overwhelm are the limiting beliefs we have grown up with, the beliefs of what we have experienced in the past and the beliefs that do not serve us anymore.

These beliefs are called CORE BELIEFS. They were instilled in childhood by our community, our families, the books we read, the things we heard, and even the television programmes we watched. So, the media, family and society play a big role in the core beliefs we have. If someone has a core belief that no matter what they were going through, they can make it, that they were strong and resourceful, that positive core belief would come up strong. They will remember that they are resourceful. They will remember that they will come through this.

However, in a scenario where someone's core beliefs are that of 'I am not worthy. I am not good enough. Bad things always happen to me. Nobody loves me, I do not deserve to be here. I am really screwed up' or even sometimes something more vulgar. When difficulties pop up those predominant thoughts would be expressed.

This is not to cast blame on your family, your friends or whatever you were exposed to growing up. This is to make you aware of those beliefs that have been subconsciously implanted into you and enable you to recognise if they are serving you or not.

What weare going to go through is how to recognise them and how to modify them if they can be modified, or eliminate them altogether and create beliefs that serve you.

I know that some had traumatic childhoods and I really do empathise with such experiences. I would; however, like to say though; your past does not necessarily have to be your future. What happened in the past is not written indelibly, never to be changed.

You are the architect of your life. You are the script writer of what happens from now on. You can rewrite that story. You have got the pen in your hand. You are the one to identify who you are.

So if you have in the past said things like me, 'I am a failure. I am unworthy. What is wrong with me?', I understand. But that doesn't have to be the case. You can make a decision today by identifying who you really are.

TASKS

Step 1- Identifying your beliefs.

A great way of recognising your core belief is to focus your attention on what your emotional reaction to situations is.

For example, if someone cuts you off in traffic, or someone is being mean to you at work, how do you respond? What happens with your body? Write this down.

Do you feel your heart racing? Do you feel your muscles going tense? Do you feel chest tightness or chest pain?

Take a few minutes to feel the feeling to perceive the sensation without trying to change it. As you feel these things in your body, ask yourself what belief goes with this. Pay attention to the response. When these beliefs come up, write them down. As you write them down, you will begin to uncover those subconscious beliefs that you have.

Step2 is to analyse each belief you have written.

Ask yourself, 'when did I start to have this belief?' This process might require you to go back into childhood. As you do so, it would help you to recognise the circumstance or scenario during which time this belief was formed.

Step 3 How do I see myself now?

This is you seeing yourself as you are through your own limiting beliefs or core beliefs, thoughts, and experiences. Write them down.

Step 4,

If those beliefs of who you are, how you see yourself now are not empowering, ask yourself this question: 'What are the positive opposites of this perception of who I am?' and write them down. An example is if you said I am a failure. The positive opposite of that is I am a success. If your statement was I am unworthy, your positive opposite will be I am worthy.

I would like to bring to your attention the importance and the power in the two words 'I AM'. These are the most powerful words in the English language because the words that follow I AM can make or break you. They can build or destroy. They are the ones that make people able to achieve or make people retreat into apathy and even death.

DECLARATION

Put your hand on your heart and say I (say your name) am worthy, I am Wonderful, I am enough. Make at least three declarations and you can use some of the positive opposites in the above exercise to replace any negative perceptions you have of yourself as the extra declarations to make about three to five declarations.

ACTION STEPS

Get your journal and write out those positive declarations.

Write out these positive declarations on post-it notes and paste them around the house.

Put them on your mirror, and on your dashboard. Put little notes of the positive declarations in your purse.

CHAPTER FOUR- FORGETTING WHO YOU ARE

I remember watching this beautiful cartoon by Pixar called 'Finding Dory'. And it was about this blue tang fish, who had lost her memory and did not know how to get back home. She didn't know much about herself, but she knew that she wasn't where she was supposed to be.

There was a discussion between her and the Stingray as he was taking them on a field trip. He made this very interesting announcement. 'Today is Stingray migration day.' While she was asking questions to find out a bit more about it, she was told that it was the day the stingrays were migrating home.

She asked, 'how would they know where home is?' He said, 'it's the instinct' and he went further to explain that 'this is that thing deep inside of you, that inner knowing'.

That is something we all have.

Sometimes when we become mums and take on all the many roles, we forget who we are. We forget our true essence. We feel busy with all the tasks that need to be done, and do not pay attention to that instinct- that inner knowing. This causes us to lose track of ourselves, to forget about filling our cup, to forget about caring for ourselves, so that we will be able to care for others.

That is when overwhelm begins to creep in. It is not our fault. We are biologically programmed as mums, to put others first, especially our children.

For example, we have the hormone, Oxytocin, which helps you to build the bond between you and your child. By the time you give birth to your child, you have got the deep desire to nourish and care for this child even if it is uncomfortable for you.

When you look at the child, you are filled with joy. Even if he or she pees on you, you do not mind. You get so excited when the child makes any sound and you worry when the child is crying because you do not want the child to be uncomfortable. This great biological arrangement within our system makes us as mothers to put the nourishment and care of our children before ours.

Of course, there are some exceptions. But that does not negate the fact we have got this circulating hormone that supports us and helps us to nourish our children. So it is no surprise that as we continue to nourish and care for our children, we sometimes forget ourselves. We forget to connect with friends, socialise, sleep, do the things we loved to do before we became mums because there is another human in our lives, who we need to nourish.

We all have 24 hours in a day. However, in that 24 hours you have got the care of the children, your partner, work, and probably your side hustle or your business, which take up most of your time. With younger children, you may find yourself unable to get a routine in place which contributes to the unpredictable nature of a typical day.

This may get more predictable when they start school and you can sort of make a plan around their schedule e.g. the school hours, or the activities they take part in after school. Even then, it might be a challenge to fit in the activities you used to do. In that case, something has to give.

And whenever something has to give, you go through a bargaining process and by elimination, you let go of those things you used to do, who you used to be and who you have always been. That is how we forget ourselves gradually until the memory of ourselves becomes so distant.

Sometimes it is not only becoming a mother that makes you forget yourself. It can happen in platonic and intimate relationships, especially when you are the 'giving party' in the relationship or in a toxic relationship where manipulation and abuse become a contributing factor.

This can be draining and has led many to states of anxiety, overwhelm and depression. When you go through unpleasant events or challenging situations, you might forget yourself.

But it doesn't have to be this way. How do I know that? Because there are many people who have been through challenging situations and they have come through on the other side, feeling more empowered. They are amazing role models for many of us.

I recall when I was crying pretty much every day after my father died. I couldn't understand why he died. I was asking the wrong question. 'Why?', hoping for an answer or better still a reversal of the event.

While I absolutely agree with the fact that when you want to get answers, you need to ask questions, asking the right questions is so important.

When I found myself asking 'why', I was not getting any response that was made sense and that made me sink deeper into despair and pain. I became a shadow of myself so much so that my physical, emotional and mental reflections did not look like me at all. In hindsight, I realised that I was asking the wrong question and getting lost in the grief.

On the day I made a decision to find a way to make this persistent overwhelm become a thing of the past, the questions I asked changed. When I started asking the right questions, I started moving forward.

Have you found yourself lost in an event or situation past or present? Have you found it to be emotionally draining or mentally overwhelming?

This is a place where you can forget who you are. As we go through this journey together, I will show you how I was able to remember who I am and look to who I am becoming.

One of the people who contributed to that progress I made in breaking free from overwhelm was Edith Edgar, an amazing lady who though I have never met her in person reframed my thinking process in her book, 'The choice'.

She survived the Holocaust during which time she experienced incredible loss.

In spite of her loss and painful experiences, she was able to go and visit Auschwitz, where the memories of all she went through came flooding back. She made a choice on how to look at it and showed us how. That is the reason why I say to you, though we might have had difficult paths, faced challenges along the way, incurred some irretrievable losses, we can choose our next path.

We can define who we are, who we are becoming and who we need to be in our journey to become our better selves.

I'm happy that you have picked up this book because not only does it tell you about the journey we as mums go through, but it also uncovers things about overwhelm, exhaustion, its causes and how you can start to discover yourself.

You can start like Dory to connect with your instincts, that inner knowing, that thing deep inside of you. It will tell you where home is, where to turn, and show you your inner superpowers. The inner knowing would help you remember who you are. This inner knowing will help you uncover who you are becoming.

I remember watching a scene in the cartoon, the *Lion King*, when Mufasa, Simba's father appeared to him after he died. Simba thought his father's death was his fault and had run away from his kingdom.

In this scene, he was contemplating returning to his kingdom after hearing news of the deplorable state the kingdom was in. However, he was afraid.

As his father spoke with him, he ended with his voice that echoes in my mind till today 'Remember who you are, Remember, Remember...'

Even if as a mum, you have forgotten who you are because of your many roles. I am saying to you today, remember, remember who you are.

CHAPTER FIVE- UNCOVERING WHO YOU ARE

'Knowing yourself is the beginning of all wisdom.' - Aristotle

This statement was true so many years ago and is still true now. When we truly know ourselves, we can live free from the factors that limit us. We can tap into the wisdom that lies both within us and around us. We can be connected to infinite intelligence and create the life we desire and deserve. This is the moment when we can fully use our superpowers and do the extraordinary.

Like the surfaces of a well cut diamond, we have got different aspects which make up who we are. We are not made up of just the body; we are made up of soul, mind and spirit. These are all connected and need to work in harmony for our holistic wellbeing.

Each aspect of our being is meant to be nourished for the others to thrive.

Imagine the wheel of a unicycle which has 2 spokes running at right angles to each other, intersecting in the middle thereby giving rise to 4 sections. The tyre of the unicycle wheel appears to have 4 curved arcs linked together. If at any point, one of these arcs is deflated, the ride on the unicycle will be very bumpy.

If; however, you wish to have a smooth ride, each of the 4 arcs making up the wheel of the unicycle need to be well inflated in harmony with the others. These 4 arcs represent the four aspects of our being- spirit, mind, soul, and body.

SPIRIT

This is an important aspect of our being. It is not physical and sometimes there is a temptation to ignore it. We need to realise, like Pierre Teilhard de Chardin said, "We are not human beings having a spiritual experience; we are spiritual beings having a human experience." This really helps us define our identity.

The spirit is what connects us to God, to our purpose, to source. The spirit is what uplifts us at those critical moments where everything else would have failed. The spirit is what connects us as humans, as people in this world.

When we think about our spiritual journey, we need to recognise what stage we are in our growth and what we need to ensure continued growth. That involves nourishment and nurturing intentionally.

For our spiritual nourishment, we should be aware of our needs. Our needs could range from: the need for meaning and purpose in our lives, the need to love and feel loved, the need to feel a sense of belonging, the need to feel hope, peace and gratitude.

As mums, we tend to pour into everyone. Even as we guide our children on their spiritual path we forget to consistently fill ourselves up. The spiritual nourishment we require is a lifeline that should constantly be connected. Keeping that lifeline to God, our source of all life, guides us in moments of confusion and helps us uncover who we are and whose we are.

MIND

The Mind is such a powerful aspect of our being. It is where thoughts are generated, ideas are conceived and personalities are developed. 'As a man thinketh, so is he' is one of my favourite verses in the book of Proverbs and that awareness is what helps us to uncover who we are as we use our minds. Our minds generate thoughts automatically which could either be negative, or positive.

The need to be mindful of the words we say to ourselves and the thoughts we dwell on cannot be overemphasized. When I was unable to do what I wanted to because I felt overwhelmed and exhausted, I spoke to myself in the harshest way. The negative statements were aimed at my identity. I used phrases like 'I am a failure'. 'I am such a bad mother.' These thoughts and words that go through our mind can be debilitating.

In the section on beliefs in chapter 3, I covered the questions we need to ask ourselves when we are faced with automatic negative thoughts or like Dr. Daniel Amen describes them, **ANTs**.

Do revisit and use this as an exercise to reframe your thoughts. Our thoughts of who we are become our reality.

Occasionally, our thoughts can be a result of the projected thoughts of others. That is why we need to be mindful of whom and what we listen to. Are we feeding ourselves with empowering content or disempowering content?

"Watch your thoughts, they become your words; watch your words, they become your actions; watch your actions, they become your habits; watch your habits, they become your character; watch your character, it becomes your destiny." — Lao Tzu

If you are in a state of overwhelm, there are a couple of things you can start to incorporate into your life. One of them is being more mindful.

Mindfulness is so critical to harmony in our being. When we practise mindfulness in relation to our thoughts, we become more aware of our thoughts- recognising and acknowledging them in the present moment.

Even if you look in the mirror and you are disappointed by what you see either as a result of what you have done or what you have not done, recognise the greatness within you. Tap into your inner super mum because that is who you are. Your past does not equate to your future.

SOUL

The soul is the seat of our emotions. Our emotions link to our energy vibrations. The more positive our emotions are, the higher our energy vibrations.

Our most dominant emotions can attract people to us or repel people from us. It can also attract positive or negative realities too.

In a state of emotional overwhelm, we may occasionally forget who we are and express our identity based on what we feel at the moment. When we feel fear, shame or guilt, we express the identity of not being enough.

When we feel sad or depressed, we may express the identity of being unworthy.

This shows the interconnectedness of each aspect of our being. We can also uncover who we are by being aware of our spirit, mind, soul and body. What I have found is that the journey of self-discovery starts by asking the right questions.

The nourishment of our soul is so important because when we are filled up and well nourished, we can experience peace, joy and fulfilment.

Like Leon Brown stated, "You must be the master of your emotions if you wish to live in peace, for he who can control himself becomes free."

BODY

The body is the earthenware vessel which serves as a house for us during our earthly journey. It comes to life when we have breath and the spirit within us. Just like in nature, our body also has the elements- air, fire, water and earth contained in it. We need to recognise how these elements work in harmony with each other.

Recognising that the processes of our body work in a cyclical pattern helps us appreciate who we are and how we can enhance who we are becoming by our daily practices.

As a result, we need to take steps to ensure nourishment that comes through food, the strengthening that comes through exercise, the cleanliness that comes through washing and general grooming among the other things that our bodies need.

We are constantly evolving. Things are constantly changing and the ability to recognise who we are, and who we are becoming in the midst of the changes is paramount to unlocking our superpowers. These changes are inevitable and serve as seeds for our evolution. They can be internal changes or external changes.

When faced with an adverse situation (external change), we respond with internal changes to each aspect of our being. Let me give you a personal example of how each aspect of our being can be affected. When my father died a few years ago, I experienced a tsunami of emotions- fear, anger, guilt, deep sadness and the many expressions of grief.

These emotions emanated from my soul following the loss. The effects did not stop there. I had a lot of automatic negative thoughts constantly in my mind. These thoughts fed the guilt, the fear and overwhelm that I was experiencing, at the time. They also made me question my faith, my values and beliefs.

I was spiritually withdrawn and found it difficult to pray. I found myself asking questions like: 'Why did God let this happen?' I started to lose hope and the clouds were so grey every single day. It did not end there. I had poor sleep, lost three dress sizes and felt tired all the time and forgot who I was. Can you see how that external factor (the death of my father) affected my soul, mind, spirit and body?

Have you ever felt this way when something happened in your life? Have you felt like you do not know who you are anymore?

CHAPTER SIX- WHAT'S ALL THE FUSS ABOUT? (CAUSES OF OVERWHELM)

I looked around me, the room was dark. My alarm had rung a while ago and I had switched it off. It looked as though I had been up all night. I hadn't slept a wink. I lay there staring at the ceiling, trying to gather enough energy to move. My usual first thing to do would have been to turn on some music. I usually listen to music in the morning to get myself out of bed, singing and being thankful for a new day.

But on that day, I just didn't have the strength, or the ability to remember to turn on some music. This was one of those dreary mornings when I was stuck in bed but it was not the only one. Eventually another alarm rang. This alarm was for quarter to seven. Oh my goodness, I jumped out of bed. I had to get the children ready and off to nursery.

So while panicking, I got the bags ready, woke them up and started to run around putting things together. After a quick shower and getting dressed, I made porridge for them on the hob. So while they had breakfast, I loaded the buggy with the bags and attached the ride on board. I only had a few minutes to drop them off at school before I had to get to work.

It was so cold and I wasn't driving at the time. I looked outside and saw that it was snowing. 'Oh no', I thought to myself, 'it's snowing again today'. The snow on the floor was about half an inch, which was not too bad. So I put the children's coats, scarves, gloves and hats on and then mine, strapped the little one in the buggy while his sister hopped onto the ride-on board.

As I pushed the buggy, the flakes of snow falling became clumps, making it hard to see. 'Oh no', I thought to myself 'How could this be happening now?' It became heavier so I had the rain cover over the buggy. My daughter, who was standing on the board, was being hit despite having her hood up, and her gloves and hats in place.

So I thought to myself I will use the rain cover to cover her too. So she bent over a little and was covered by the rain cover as well. As I pushed the buggy on the slippery pavement due to some melted snow from the night before, I was going downhill. I needed to be extra careful not to let go or slip and not to make any mistake.

Then halfway through the walk, I thought to myself, 'did I turn off the hob?' Panic set in. My heart started racing. At that moment I thought to myself, 'I can't go back now. I have to drop the children off.' I started to blame myself. 'If only you had just gotten up early and said your morning prayers, this wouldn't be happening'. And as usual there was that mean voice in my head saying all kinds of hurtful things. Things I wish not to remember.

How many times do we do something or fail to do something which gets us worried or upset?

How easily is it for that self-critical voice to come out and give us a high school type washing down?

Often, we speak to ourselves in ways that we would not talk to our friends or even our enemies.

After dropping them off, I ran uphill with the snow on my face. I felt weak, tired, and totally exhausted. I was running late for work but I had to check that the hob was switched off. Thank goodness it was switched off. I didn't want to burn the place down.

So I grabbed my bag and went to work. As we prepared for the ward round, I had a few tasks I needed to do. The overwhelm I felt was beyond words. I am not sure if anybody saw it on my face, but I knew that I felt it.

Have you been in that situation where so many things are going on, you have so many tasks to complete and you are so pressed for time?

Have you felt like you are not good enough and you start blaming yourself?

Are there times when you were criticised on all sides- by others and yourself?

I did that quite a bit. While I was not looking for sympathy, it is something I needed to recognise and be mindful of. So, what causes the overwhelm we experience? As some would say, 'what's the fuss all about?'

Overwhelm has been described as being buried or drowned beneath a huge massof something. That is the way we sometimes feel; as though we have been buried or are drowning with so many things happening in our life. We go through different situations or events that could cause us to feel this way.

While it may not always be referred to as feeling overwhelmed, other words used to describe the feeling include: being swarmed, inundated, overloaded, or snowed under.

Which one are you using to describe what you are feeling?

Sometimes we may not even have the words to describe what we feel, but we know it is there.

When we hear the word overwhelm, it can have a negative connotation. At work, we do not want to tell anyone that we are feeling overwhelmed. Partly, because we feel that people would look down on us, as though we are incompetent and unable to cope. We feel shame and guilt. This can lead to fear of real or imagined consequences.

In sufficiently agitated situations where we feel frustrated, anger many ensue. All this stems from the social stigma that surrounds overwhelm. There are many thoughts and feelings we experience, but we keep quiet about it and don't say a word. We also are reluctant to seek help until it gets too much.

It is very important to know the causes of overwhelm so that we can pay attention to them. I would discuss these causes in 4 main parts.

1. **Physical causes of overwhelm**

This can be the presence of a lot of work to do especially when there are deadlines that have passed or are fast approaching. It is good to have deadlines because they get things done. But when you have so many that have not been met and demands are high, they can cause overwhelm, at work or even in our personal life.

One thing that helps is to understand the concept of the Time management matrix for productivity. We have got the things that are important and things that are urgent.

This matrix is divided in quadrants:

Quadrant 1- Important and urgent

Quadrant 2- Important but not urgent

Quadrant 3- Not important but urgent

Quadrant 4- Not important and not urgent

You will find details of this in most productivity books so I am not going to go into so much detail. However, from a holistic point of view I would like to draw your attention to common activities that can fit into these quadrants and why we get distracted even though we know we have so much to do.

TIME MANAGEMENT MATRIX

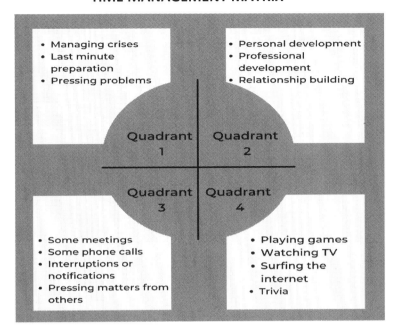

Quadrant 1 (the important and urgent) tasks are those which have a deadline that has passed or is fast approaching and may have some consequences if not done. They were not always in this quadrant. They came as a result of last minute realisations that they exist or postponing on taking action on important but non urgent tasks.

Quadrant 2 (Important but non-urgent) refers to those activities that contribute to our wellbeing- physically, spiritually, mentally, emotionally, socially, financially, that deepen our connection to ourselves and others. It usually requires consistent action. When these are not done, they move into Quadrant 1 and become a source of overwhelm with far reaching consequences.

Quadrant 3 (Urgent but not important) activities are usually from someone else e.g. our children, spouse, boss, business partner etc. They usually pass on a task that is important to them

43

that needs to be attended to urgently. Sometimes we can pass it back, but most of the time we do them because of our relationship with those who gave them to us.

Quadrant 4 (the non-urgent and non-important) activities are those we use to relax or de-stress. They are not usually productive activities but are crucial, nonetheless. This is because when we have some quadrant 4 activities, we can use that as downtime to recharge and get back to being more productive.

There is however the tendency when we have so many quadrant 1 activities, that we can default into a state of panic and find ourselves doing quadrant 4 activities like surfing the internet, playing games, watching Netflix, or the kind of things that really don't move the needle in our lives. This can be a sign of self-resignation, or as though you have given up.

What usually happens is, there is a difficulty in planning our activities. This involves not scheduling the important things, especially the quadrant two tasks over time leading to them mounting up in quadrant 1.

Other physical causes include: ill health, hormone imbalance, time constraints etc. When you are ill, it can present with pain or weakness in the body or in many other ways which you might describe to a family, friend or even your doctor. These may prevent you from performing as usual and can present with features of overwhelm.

When you are feeling overwhelmed, you find yourself being forgetful, more irritable as your stress level rises. When your stress level goes up, your body responds. There is a chemical called Cortisol. It is produced in the adrenals which sit right on top of your kidneys.

Cortisol is a useful hormone, which helps you get ready for the day, and in the mornings is usually the highest. As you progress through the day, the levels drop. However, in a state of persistent stress or overwhelm, your body produces more cortisol to help you cope with that stress.

When cortisol is high, it puts you in a hyper alert state and your body responds accordingly with high blood pressure, muscle weakness, skin changes and mood swings. When you are in hyper alert mode, your body releases other chemicals such as adrenaline that cause you to get ready for a fight, flight or freeze response.

At that point, you are focused on surviving that situation rather than looking at the big picture. Blood flow is prioritised to the parts of the body required for the automatic response and diverted from non-essential activities like digestion hence this can cause bloating, changes in bowel habits or nausea and some of the features seen in irritable bowel syndrome (IBS).

We only have 24 hours in a day. While I understand that it is a limited time there are some people who get more done and do not feel overwhelmed as easily as we do.

What do they do differently? What special powers have they got?

In later chapters, we would explore some of the practices these people have incorporated into their lives that make it seem so effortless.

In a high stress condition, we find that our blood sugar is increased, to enable us to keep up with persistent demands. In the presence of high levels of blood sugar, insulin, the chemical that normally would store excess sugar, struggles a little bit and so might not function as well. This is seen in type 2 diabetes.

High levels of cortisol have also been linked to suppressed immune response which makes you susceptible to illnesses like colds, or even contagious diseases. As I mentioned before, high blood pressure may be developed thereby increasing the risk of heart attack, or stroke.

So you see how stress and overwhelm can lead to ill health and vice versa.

2. Emotional cause of overwhelm

This can be due to a loss of someone, a relationship, an opportunity, a job, or a sense of self. When there is loss, there is grief. That is where our emotions come into play- sadness, anger, fear, confusion, frustration. All the emotions start to swell up. Sometimes they are not as intense, but sometimes they come like a tsunami.

That is something I experienced quite a bit. It can also come in waves and occasionally when approaching certain days such as an anniversary. Some triggers include music, food, a smell, or sound. When these emotions feel overwhelming, we can be more anxious, experience low mood and dip into depression.

It has been particularly difficult for many people during the pandemic because there was a lot of loss. Loss of jobs, relationships, freedom to move around and go out to places that you would want to go, physical contact, social connection, financial stability and the list goes on. As a result, many people struggled with the emotional overwhelm that came with it.

Mums most especially had to think about working from home, while home-schooling and taking care of the home. Prior to this, we knew that when the children were in school, we had between 9am and 2pm or 3pm, depending on when your child's school ends to get your tasks done. With the shift to home-schooling, you not only became a teacher but also a dinner lady and snack lady who was pestered every hour for something to eat and complaints of being bored or tired.

3. **Mental causes of overwhelm.**

This is where we have a myriad of thoughts. Dr. Daniel Amen has a very unique term for describing negative thoughts. He calls them ANTs (Automatic Negative Thoughts). Some of these thoughts are due to what people have said to us or what we say to ourselves consistently. They are the thoughts that keep going on in our minds causing us to worry, or question ourselves.

Our brain is designed to ensure that we survive any threats. The survival brain is still as active now as it was millennia ago where it helped our ancestors to stay alive. However, when we are faced with conditions that are not life-threatening but your survival brain perceives it as such, you go into panic mode and leave out rational thinking. Sometimes these thoughts can be debilitating. They have been the cause of people self-harming, self-medicating or even committing suicide.

As I mentioned before, whenever you want to solve a problem, you need to ask the right questions. Facing our ANTs is so important. This would help us challenge the negative thoughts and get us from that state of overwhelm or feeling submerged to a state of clarity. This gives your thinking brain the ability to solve problems by logical thinking.

So I'm going to delve into those questions you can ask when challenging the negative thoughts.

Qa. Is this true? You need to ask, Is it really true? You need to also clarify if this is fact or fiction.

Qb. How does this thought make me feel?

Qc. How would it feel if I did not have this thought?

Qd. What would happen if I swapped this negative thought for the positive opposite? That helps you to deal with overwhelm, that gets you into a state of paralysis, anxiety, or withdrawal.

4. Social cause of overwhelm

This includes but is not restricted to the people around us such as family, friends, colleagues, social media, media influences, societal practices and culture which contribute to our conditioning.

So our upbringing, our social network, and the people we connect to or aspire to connect to play a key role.

Social factors that can contribute to overwhelm can come in the form of comparison with our peers. Others can include our social status and achievements. There is also the trend of putting our best pictures on social media which feigns perfection whereas we might be living in chaos or wishing our lives were like the picturesque images seen on Instagram or other social media platforms.

Another common response to social causes of overwhelm is a trip to the land of envy, guilt or regret. Other social causes are the presence of trolls who bring up such vile comments, accusations or opinions. While it is easy to say 'just ignore them, they are not worth your time,' I would say that it does have an impact. Knowing how to deal with such will prevent you from getting overwhelmed or reverse the overwhelm you are feeling.

We are subjected to this because we are social animals; we crave approval, recognition and community. We associate with people who we share a common bond with or interest. In situations where our place in the community is threatened, we get stressed, agitated, frustrated and then overwhelmed.

Some people went through a financial difficulty and as a result, they experienced a drop in their income level.

Can they still associate with their peers who are meeting in the local clubs talking about millions and billions that they are earning and how their companies are thriving?

There is a possibility that they might isolate themselves, have feelings of pain, shame or worry and that takes them down the route of overwhelm.

However, given the right focus, they would be able to activate the problem-solving functioning part of their brain and make decisions that would make a positive difference for them.

We are the ones who can make these decisions that will break us free from overwhelm. The answers do not come from far away. It comes from a conscious search from deep within.

CHAPTER SEVEN- WHERE DID ALL MY ENERGY GO?

I couldn't move not because I did not want to. I didn't have the energy to think or do anything. In addition, my muscles did not want to respond to my will. Thank goodness my breathing and the beating of my heart are automatic. If not, there might have been a problem with having to force them to act and keep me alive.

This was a daily occurrence that kept me flawed and unable to do the things that I usually enjoyed doing. I was so thankful for that fateful day when I got tired of feeling tired all the time. I had to find out what was causing it and fix it.

This is such a common feature that mums experience on a daily basis and the causes are varied and multiple. Our body is always speaking to us. Initially, it whispers to us and when we do not act, it starts to whimper with the hope that we respond. If however at that point we do not respond, it starts to scream and shout.

When we start to feel tired all the time, that is the stage at which our body is screaming. Rather than just put some band aid on it, it would be great to identify the underlying causes and take action to eliminate or reverse them.

That is the main reason why in this book, I will be looking into the causes as well as the effects or the symptoms you express.

Exhaustion has been described as a state of extreme physical or mental tiredness. In addition to that, we have also seen that it goes beyond physical strain, mental tiredness, or emotional drain. Sometimes, feeling burnt out has been used as an expression of what is happening to mums.

Feeling exasperated is also another way of describing that state of exhaustion. When you feel exhausted, you are at a higher risk for developing illnesses and you have reduced immune response.

The causes of exhaustion include:

1. **Physical causes**

There are many physical causes. However, I will cover the ones I consider common and apply to most people. This list is not exhaustive. The aim is to ensure that the causes identified can be corrected easily even if you have a busy schedule. One cause of exhaustion is lack of food or the consumption of the wrong type of food for you.

Eating certain foods causes inflammation in our gut. This process includes swelling, heat, pain, and loss of function which could lead to poor absorption of nutrients and cell death. Foods that you are allergic to or intolerant of can cause this.

Another physical cause is when there is an imbalance in chemicals that regulate body function. A deficiency or excess of hormones causes imbalance which affects normal body function.

Weather and climate changes can also have an impact on our energy level. This could be due to varied exposure to sunlight across the seasons. People tend to be more energetic during summer than winter. In addition, there are some seasonal mood changes that affect our energy levels.

Inadequate hydration is another common cause which is often overlooked. We are made up of 60 to 70% of water. Water is a main constituent of blood which serves as the medium of transport within the body. It also is a source of hydrogen ions which are responsible for the level of acidity in the body (measured in pH).

Because of the many chemical processes occurring in the body all the time, maintaining the optimal temperature and pH is essential.

The ideal pH for optimal body function is between 7.35 and 7.45. The balance is maintained by the kidneys, gut and lungs. Our level of hydration contributes to this balance.

In essence we need to ensure adequate hydration. When brain cells are dehydrated, we could experience features like brain fog, confusion, tiredness, and headache.

2. **Emotional causes of exhaustion.**

Apart from the seasons that can cause mood changes, there are multiple factors that can cause various expressions of emotion.

Emotions are expressed as energy vibrations. We have higher vibration emotions like empowerment, peace, joy, and love. The low level vibration emotions include apathy, shame, guilt and grief.

The mid-level vibration emotions include anger, pride, from where you can move higher into some areas of positivity, like courage or being neutral, and then acceptance.

These are very useful ways of viewing emotional causes of exhaustion. When we express positive emotions we feel more energetic. However, with negative emotions, we have lower energy vibrations and as such feel exhausted.

One of the many books I read, going through my period of grief, was an amazing book by David R. Hawkins *Letting Go*.

That book expressed the vibrations we have as human beings. Our energy levels depend on the emotion we were expressing at any given time. We should therefore be mindful of our emotions. The soul is the seat of our emotions. In the later chapters we will explore how we can nourish our souls so the emotions expressed are at a higher vibration level.

3. **Mental causes of exhaustion.**

As mentioned in the previous chapter, we have a constant flow of automatic thoughts. They could be positive or negative thoughts. When there is an increase in the number of negative thoughts, such as self-loathing, guilt, or not being enough, they translate into negative feelings which are at lower energy levels. When these negative thoughts are persistent they can cause mentally exhaustion. It can present with difficulty concentrating, solving problems or maintaining focus.

That can cause us to either make the wrong decision or make no decision at all. Sometimes, we may be more inclined to do non-urgent and unimportant tasks rather than attend to the urgent and important or the non-urgent but important tasks which serve as building blocks for our overall well-being.

4. Spiritual causes of exhaustion.

We are spiritual beings having a human experience. As such we need to maintain a healthy spiritual connection. I bring this up because we did not just come into being by accident or because we decided to be created. I know many people have different beliefs. However, there is immense evidence in the existence of a power, force, infinite intelligence, God who governs all.

My belief is that we were created by a loving God in his image and likeness. The aim of our existence is for us to grow, live abundantly in this world and enjoy enhanced connection and fellowship with God now and for eternity.

The moment there is a disruption in this spiritual connectedness, we feel exhausted.

Many sages and spiritual leaders have gone days or weeks without the usual physical nourishment that gives energy while they were on a quest for spiritual enlightenment and during that period of connectedness they felt they had even more energy. In many religions, a disruption in this spiritual connection is caused by sin.

Sin is a vice, a disobedience to a rule, or a code of conduct as specified by God. The process of regaining connection involves repentance from the wrongdoing, and asking for forgiveness. That reconnection enhances our energy so we feel like we are living the purpose for which we were made and can live the life of abundance we desire and deserve. When we find ourselves exhausted, sometimes it could be as a result of a spiritual detachment.

5. Financial causes of exhaustion.

Have you ever been stressed or had low energy because you saw your negative bank balance or a pile of bills? That is a typical example of how finances or the lack thereof can cause depletion in our energy levels. Remember Ava from chapter 3!

6. Social causes of exhaustion

Humans crave connection. In ancient times, whenever someone violated a major societal rule, he was either sent away on exile or locked up in prison. Even in modern times, we have prisons or correctional facilities. There is the isolation confinement reserved for offenders within these facilities. Separation from others can be a painful experience.

During the pandemic, when our human contact was limited, many people felt exhausted and lacking energy.

Another way to look at social causes of exhaustion is that being in close contact with people who have a negative impact on your mood can cause us to feel depleted.

While I discuss the causes of feeling exhausted, it is also important to pay attention to the way our bodies expresses exhaustion. Being able to pick up on the subtle signs that our bodies always tell us is so important. By recognising them we can take the required action to break free from feeling overwhelmed and exhausted.

CHAPTER 8- TAKING NOTE OF THE SIGNS

It was my birthday and I was not ready for it. I particularly love celebrating my birthday. Usually I would have planned a special meal, what to wear, and fun activities for the day whether celebrating solo or with others. However, this time around, I did not feel like there was anything worth celebrating. 'This was another workday', I thought. So I dressed up and was heading into work. As I walked past the mirror, I looked at myself. I looked like a skeleton that had clothes thrown on it. My heart sank. 'How did I become like this?' I looked tired. I felt exhausted. That was the first time I took note of the signs.

Our body is always communicating with us. Initially it is in whispers which appear as subtle signs. If we do not pay attention, it starts to whimper and if this is not noticed, it starts to scream and shout. Many times we need to notice what is going on before it gets to a point where our body is screaming and shouting at us.

Our bodies are an exquisite piece of machinery which have a complex yet connected internal operating system. It also communicates with the external environment by taking information through our senses- **sight, hearing, touch, taste, smell and our sixth sense**, processing it and giving an appropriate response at the time. Its aim is to ensure harmony and fluidity of communication and processes so that we not only survive, but thrive.

In this chapter, we would cover the subtle signs that your body communicates to you and how you can increase your ability to notice them so that you take action sooner.

However, when the body tells us to respond in a way and we either do not listen or postpone taking action because of the many roles we have, it takes a toll and can manifest as overwhelm and exhaustion. This can lead to DIS-EASE.

For the purpose of recognising the signs, we would focus on our senses. The first time I learned about the senses was in primary school where we had a chart with pictures of the eyes, nose, ears, tongue, and hands. We also recited some text like 'I can see with my eyes, I can smell with my nose, I can taste with my tongue, I can feel with my hand, I can hear with my ears.' Those were the phrases that went with the pictures and they stuck with me for a long time.

As I progressed in my learning journey, the concept of our senses expanded especially in medical school to the minute details of the anatomy and physiology which explored receiving and processing impulses to a form of information that can be understood and transmitted. In my personal growth journey, the knowledge of the sixth sense was explained even though I had experienced it many times before.

Understanding how these senses work creats a deeper understanding of the connection between the body, soul, mind, and spirit.

SIGHT

The sense of sight goes beyond the use of our eyes. When we look around, there are many things to see, however there are a few that catch out attention. This is a protective quality to prevent us from information overload. The things that get our attention can be related to what we are thinking about,

what someone points out to us or

what appears unusual.

a. **What we are thinking about**

Have you ever thought about getting a new coat or dress and suddenly you see it everywhere you go? That is the effect of selective attention that the reticular activating system provides. It helps us to see things we are looking for.

So if you have negative thoughts in your mind, you attention will be drawn to see things going wrong around you to align with your thoughts.

In moments of overwhelm, we are most times on edge or agitated and the survival state of mind is most prominent.

In that situation, we can calm our minds by using mindfulness practices which I will go into in more detail in later chapters. These practices help us to be more aware of changes in what we see and experience.

b. **What someone points out to us**

Two heads they say is better than one. Another peculiar thing about the two heads is that they have twice as many eyes. There are some things that others see that we do not see. There are many times in my clinical career when someone comes with a change in the appearance of their skin which they had not noticed, but it was picked up by another person. As mothers we also notice differences in how our child looks and we can seek advice or help to address this change.

c. What appears unusual

If you entered a room where everyone wore a red shirt and then suddenly there was someone with a white shirt, you are bound to notice. That is the same way that a rash, dark rings around your eyes, and prominent bones stand out.

There is an exercise that helps us become more aware.

This can be done in the kitchen and you can also include your kids while making it super fun.

This is the practice of mindful cooking. This is when you pay attention to each step of the cooking process- bringing out the pots and pans, washing the food, noticing what they look like before and after it is washed, cut and cooked, noticing the colours and size etc. By describing what you see, you strengthen your sense of sight and the interpretation you get from the data. This can be applied to our bodies.

SMELL

Have you ever played a game where you were blindfolded and told to note the difference between one item and another based on the use of your sense of smell? Oh, I remember when I played that game. It was particularly interesting until a pungent smell was brought close to my nose.

I want you to realize that the sense of smell is not just the physical ability to sniff and have those receptors send messages to your brain of whether it is a sweet, fruity, sour, or pungent smell.

No, it goes beyond that. It includes the absence of smell or the perception of danger.

As mums, we get a bit of practice with this particular skill because our babies initially communicate their needs by crying.

The smell of poop may indicate to you it is the cause of discomfort for the child. The moment you are able to clean the child, the child starts to smile and feel happy again because you have removed that discomfort.

And you picked up on that using your sense of smell.

For us mums we can pay attention to the smell of our urine which could be an indication of our level of hydration or the presence of an infection. Other things whose smell can give us some information include our monthly bleeds, cervical mucus and body odours.

I want you to turn that super mum nose inward.

What is that thing in your life that is giving an unpleasant odour? It could be something you are not particularly sure about but just does not feel quite right. It also does not have to be a physical smell. The sense of smell is also linked to the sixth sense and helps us to perceive danger.

Sometimes a smell might be a Deja vu experience of something we have been through. When we do not pay attention, we face the consequences. Let's pay close attention to the impulses we perceive that could indicate a big change in our lives.

TASTE

From the days of pretend play cooking scenes, I recall we would demonstrate tasting and make sounds like it was absolutely delicious. As I became more aware of the cooking that occurs in the kitchen, I noticed that as you cook, and add you ingredients you taste.

So what if you have altered taste or lose the ability to taste? These can be signs of infection, inflammation and deficiency in vitamins and minerals. Pay close attention.

One useful exercise is the practice of mindful eating. You can start doing this once a week and then more frequently if you can.

This is when you pay attention to the appearance, texture and flavours of your food. You chew intentionally, take note of the symphony of flavours in your mouth and express gratitude for how the food got there. Not only does this train our senses and make our digestion of food more efficient, but it also provides a calming and uplifting effect in our being.

TOUCH

Human beings love connection. When we reach out to touch someone as we speak it draws us close to them. There are chemicals released in our bodies that calm us down when we have a loving touch. We can perceive changes in our bodies and the environment.

One of the factors that made the pandemic quite challenging was we had to refrain from physical contact.

Not only can we feel connected by touching physically, but we can also perceive emotions by the vibration energy emitted around us. By enhancing this sense, we have increased self-awareness, situational awareness and spatial awareness.

An exercise that can be used to enhance this sense is the **BODY SCAN**. In this practice, you should be in a comfortable position, in a quiet room (if possible) and take note of the sensation you feel from the different parts of your body as you scan from head to toe. The idea is not to change what you feel, but to recognise and acknowledge it. This practice not only makes us more self-aware, but it improves our concentration and the ability to be calm.

HEARING

The ability to hear is so profound because it is a fundamental part of communication. Stephen Covey in his book '7 Habits of highly effective people', he says 'Seek first to understand...' To be able to understand, you need to listen.

Our body is always speaking to us and when we are more alert to the whispers, we are able to take action before we become unwell.

However, as mums we sometimes get busy and engulfed in our activities that we listen half-heartedly or not at all.

To overcome this, we can introduce an interesting exercise that we can do on a regular basis which enhances our sense of hearing. It sharpens our listening skills and helps you to pick up on messages we otherwise may not have noticed. This exercise is called **'MINDFUL LISTENING.'**

This exercise requires you to be in a comfortable position and pay attention to the different sounds around you while listening intently. Apart from external sounds, you might be able to pick up on internal sounds, like your heart beat or your breath.

SIXTH SENSE

Mothers are most especially endowed with the ability to pick up on the communication from the sixth sense. The inner knowing has so many layers. By peeling them off one by one, you get closer to new revelations.

Some instruments that have made me more in tune with my sixth sense are affliction, challenges and adversity.

The sixth sense is sometimes referred to as intuition or the gut feeling. It is linked to the other 5 senses (sight, smell, taste, touch, hearing) but goes beyond what many understand on the physical level. There are times when I made some decisions due to an inner knowing but could hardly produce evidence that it was the right thing to do. These feelings are not easy to explain to someone else and can often be misunderstood.

Though it is not fully understood it saves us a great deal. Some have described the sixth sense as a way we get spiritual assistance on our earthly journey. It is communicated to us even before there are apparent physical signs. The idea of visions, premonitions, Deja vu and out of body experiences come to mind when I think about this.

Before the death of my father, I might have picked up on a few subtle messages from my sixth sense before any physical signs were present but not as deeply and as frequently as I do now. Through the affliction and the pain, I become more aware as I grow.

The journey has been profound and I am learning as I go. We might be going through challenges and there is a tendency to be overwhelmed, however, being open to the guidance that your sixth sense provides is transformational.

However, when we view these challenges as opportunities to grow, we learn more about ourselves and others. We tap into the superpowers we have within. We become resourceful and create the life we desire and deserve as the supermums that we are.

CHAPTER NINE- TAKING STOCK OF WHERE YOU ARE

I was on a travel site a couple of years ago planning my next holiday. As usual, before I could plan my travel I had to put in my starting location and my destination. The suggested routes gave options of a direct flight and in some cases multiple stops before arriving at the destination. That is similar to the experience we have on our life journey.

On a journey with multiple stops like we have in our lives, we need to be aware of where we are at each time. This is so important because it helps in our preparation for the journey and gathering the much needed resources.

When you know your starting point and destination, you will be able to direct your travel intentionally and not be tossed about by every twist and turn. You will also be aware of the direction of travel, how long it is going to take, and what you need on the way.

When we talk about feeling overwhelmed and exhausted, we need to explore what level we are at. This is because someone who is struggling to run is different from someone who is struggling to stand up from the bed. The level of support and tactics that would be made available to each of them would be different.

This is the kind of important information that increased self-awareness brings. In the previous chapter, we uncovered how your various senses increase your self-awareness, situational awareness and spatial awareness. Once you are able to know where you are emotionally, spiritually, mentally, and physically you get clarity on what direction you need to go. Your awareness serves as a compass which guides you towards your desired destination.

Life communicates with us constantly. Some of us pick up on the messages by visual, auditory, tactile perception and even the sixth sense. All these ways of picking up on what life is saying, or what life is expressing to us, are so important. That helps us not only to manage and thrive through different situations, but to build awesome relationships, personally, professionally, and in every aspect of our lives.

What if you get curveballs thrown in your path?

Well! That is what happens all the time in our life journey. There are unexpected occurrences that throw our plans out the window. We need to expect them and prepare for them. We do not need to be afraid of them, but should view them as learning experiences that make us better.

As a mum, I know what it is like when travelling with the children. Before leaving the house, you need to ensure that they have been to the toilet. You also need to have food, snacks and drinks packed and some form of entertainment to last through the journey. However, no matter how carefully we plan, we can have a few curve balls thrown in our way. This can make the journey last longer or appear more challenging.

Recently, I had a road trip with my children. When we set off with all our gear prepped and ready, loaded into the car, we started heading happily in the direction of our destination. Alas, we were met with an occurrence on the way. There had been a vehicle fire and an access road had been blocked off.

As a result, there was a build-up of traffic and a lot of delays. Using my navigation system, I was looking for alternative routes that would circumvent the obstruction and get us to our destination faster.

After 5 hours, I am delighted to say that we arrived at our destination. This 2 hour 15 minute journey became a 5 hour journey. I am glad to say however that on the return journey, we did not have such challenges.

At this point, Let's take an inventory of where you are.

Here are a few questions you can ask yourself in your self-audit.

1. What is your starting point?

2. Where are you emotionally?

3. What is your energy level at different times of the day?

4. Are you prepared for the journey ahead?

It is human nature to strive for something better but to do that we need to know what is good. Then we can work to get what is better, and ultimately what is best.

So take out your journal and have a little think about what is going on. Respond to the questions above. Be honest with yourself. When you gain that clarity on where you are at the moment, there is no door that you can't open.

There is no obstacle you cannot surmount. You can move from overwhelm to calm, from complete exhaustion to being energetic, from a place of abject poverty to a place of financial abundance, from a place of total ignorance to a place of enlightenment, knowledge and understanding, from a place of ill health and debilitating disease to a place of awesome, holistic well-being.

CHAPTER 10- TAKING STOCK OF WHAT YOU HAVE

'If only we knew who we are, and what immense capacity and potential lies within us we would not live in a place of fear. '– Dr. Dunni

I attended a Tony Robbins' event where we were talking about the things that help us as humans enhance our ability to achieve great feats. The story was told about Roger Bannister. Roger Bannister is the man who showed that it was possible to run a mile in less than 4mins. Before that time, it was deemed impossible.

There were also theories about how the heart would explode if the speed required to achieve this feat was ever reached. Since Roger Bannister showed it was possible, many people have achieved this and keep breaking the world record of being the fastest.

The potential of the human being to achieve anything is infinite and unlimited. We just need to believe that it is possible and take action to move us ahead. The potential that lies within us has immense energy. This is the potential energy that sits within many of us. I like to call them superpowers because they are extraordinary and super powerful.

When we are upset most times, we do not focus on the immense abilities within us, rather we focus on the problems and challenges we face. When we focus on these challenges, they are magnified and that is what makes us overwhelmed.

The great people in history who achieved great feats faced challenges and were criticised when they voiced out the possibility of making a supposedly impossible thing, possible. But the moment they were able to go beyond that period of criticism, and even rejection, the world embraced them as achievers, pioneers, and geniuses.

That is why we as mums need to see ourselves as Supermums because that is who we are and we have so many superpowers lying within us.

In this chapter, I would like us to take stock of what we have.

Every mum has superpowers, but sometimes she might not recognise it or at times may take it for granted.

I will guide you on ways by which you can identify your unique potential which I would call your superpowers. Here are a few questions to consider:

1. Is there something that you do with ease that others find difficult to do?

2. Are you trained in a skill or do you have knowledge you have acquired?

3. Are there certain attributes that you have exhibited that have either helped you to achieve something or prevented you from getting into trouble?

4. Do you find it easy to be, to do, or to experience something that others probably don't?

These questions will guide you to identify what unique qualities you have.

You can also get a trusted friend to answer these questions for you if you are not able to assess yourself.

You might have guessed it already. I love superheroes. When I was young, my father introduced us to superheroes and being very close to my brother, we grew up watching superhero movies and reading superhero comic books. I knew pretty much every superhero at that time. It was really exciting seeing their different powers- the ability to spin the web, fly, have super strength, have laser vision, be super-fast and the list goes on.

The next thing I'd like you to take stock of is who you have.

Apart from the great potential you have within, there are also people and things you have around you that would serve as the power pack you have to break free from overwhelm and exhaustion.

There was once a street bully who picked on everyone on the street. Children were terrified to go to the corner shop to get anything, because they did not want to be bullied by him. This bully continued until one day one of the boys who lived in the neighbourhood went to the shops.

As he was coming back with the items he had bought for his parents, he was stopped by this bully. The boy confidently said, 'Leave me alone. I need to get home because my parents are expecting these items.'

As the bully continued to taunt him, the boy said, 'I will call my parents who will deal with you accordingly.' The boy's parents were well-known. His father was a police officer and his mum was the head teacher at the local school. Instantly, the bully left him alone.

I would like to ask, who do you have in your corner?

Who are your friends or family members who have got your back?

Who are those people you can depend on?

They could be your mentors, colleagues, coaches, neighbours, and team members. Those are the people you can delegate tasks to. They can help you in challenging moments. Sometimes they could even be strangers. So many times on my journey, strangers have helped me.

Many times we feel like we can do everything. However, life is not meant to be done alone. We are meant to work together. We are meant to utilise our collective strengths to uplift each other. To do that we need to recognise our superpowers and share with others. We also need to allow others to use their superpowers to support, empower and uplift us. This is the essence of the cycle of life. So, go ahead, ask for help and receive help.

I struggled with asking for help for a long time and I still have to consciously accept help when it is offered and ask when it is needed. We need this as mums so our cup is filled and our being is restored to fullness.

Do I hear someone say, I cannot find any superpowers I have or anyone around me?

If that is you, I have got you covered. The solution to that is the power of **resourcefulness**. Your ability to be resourceful is what makes a huge difference in our lives. If someone has resources but no resourcefulness, the resources can vanish in flash and she would be left with nothing. However, resourcefulness is such a skill that can be learned and taught and is a lifeline for us as mums.

Resourcefulness is what helps us to move from a place of overwhelm to a place of hope and possibility. Resourcefulness is what makes us respond positively in the midst of adversity. Resourcefulness is what gets us from a point of pain to a point of gain and growth. As we express that resourcefulness and practice it, it becomes automatic and easier to do. We can also teach your children to be resourceful. Being resourceful is an amazing skill that makes a huge difference in our lives.

In the following sections, I have discussed the superpowers that I used to break free from the feeling of overwhelm and exhaustion. You would be able to explore which one resonates with you, or which one stands out to you. What I have done with the superpowers is not to name them, but to describe what they do in a continuous tense.

PART II- THE SUPERPOWERS

CHAPTER 11- DISRUPTING

'I have had enough', I thought, tears streaming down my cheeks. I took one more glance at my adorable children who had been strong for me early that morning. I was so proud of them. They were now fast asleep and I knew I had work to do. Tiptoeing out of the room, I closed the door behind me. Just then my heart started to race. The butterflies came alive in my belly. I went to the dining table where my laptop was open and papers covered almost half of the table. I sat down trembling.

'Where do I start,' I thought as the thoughts kept racing. I closed my eyes trying to focus on one but they eluded me. As I reached up to wipe a tear from my cheek, my hand touched the laptop which seemed to buzz to life. That almost made me jump. The thoughts seemed to freeze like multiple post-it notes on a cork board and soon they were gone. Oh my goodness, I could not believe that the sudden disruptive sound could create such an effect.

Disruption has been viewed as a disturbance or a nuisance. In this case, it was my saving grace that brought me back on track. The power of intentional disruption cannot be overlooked. When we are faced with challenges, the pressure can either make or break you. The choice is entirely yours.

When you decide that the challenge would make you, that is when you take a stand. But if you decide, to allow it to break you, you go down a very deep, downward spiral. I would therefore like to make you aware of your first superpower, THE POWER OF DISRUPTING. This power makes you unbeatable and unshakable.

Many people look at disruption as a bad word that should not be said, or heard. What makes this different from just making trouble is the intention you bring to it. It is a proactive activity rather than a reactive one.

There was a boy who was crying about how ugly the Lego building he had put together was. His dad said, 'if you do not like what you have made, stop, take it apart and start again.' Sometimes, like that child we settle in the pain and discomfort. I will always advocate for a good cry because it needs expression. However, it is also important to make a move to address the issue at hand.

The first step to getting anything done is by creating a disruption of 'what is' so that you can build 'what can be'- the goal you desire.

Whenever you want to change flour, eggs, sugar, and butter into cake, you need to cause a disruption of the individual ingredients and their surroundings. They each get transformed from their normal appearance to a more evolved one. The end product is more valuable than all the ingredients.

Society would be happy if we just sat down and did as we are told. Well, not anymore. This is the time to decide to take a stand for what you want and against what does not serve you. It may require a break from the so-called norm.

To move you from feeling overwhelmed and exhausted, we need to break some things. They include:

1. Breaking from limiting beliefs

We have discussed limiting beliefs in a previous chapter and identified how deep seated they can be. There are many professionals and experts who offer internal work. It is called internal work because it really is an internal process to uncover the deep seated, broad-based iceberg. This requires you to dig deep.

The thoughts and emotions arising from the limiting beliefs need to be expressed. You need to resist the urge to suppress or repress the emotions. The moment you are able to create that intentional disruption to break free from those internal limitations. You are truly free.

2. Breaking from expectations

The beliefs that we have about ourselves are formed when we absorb the thoughts, words, and actions of people around us. Some beliefs we have are empowering, especially those stemming from the positive reinforcement like supportive parents, teachers and peers.

However, in situations when we experience thoughts, words and actions of criticism, rejection, or abuse, we start to build limiting beliefs about ourselves. It is a very uncomfortable process, and can also be painful. That process involves breaking away the dead layers that are not allowing us to grow.

These beliefs serve as a fountain from which negative thoughts and words (I am unworthy, I am not good enough, I am not pretty enough, I am not smart enough, I am a failure, etc.) flow. In addition, we start to act in ways that sabotage our growth and progress based on the beliefs we have.

When we experience a challenge, we fail before we start because we do not believe we can surmount it.

These causes are overwhelming and serve as a negative reinforcement of the undesired manifestation. It is therefore crucial to break the limiting beliefs and replace them. The reason why you need to replace them is that nature abhors a vacuum.

If you just break them and clear the space without filling the space with empowering beliefs, they will sprout and grow even faster just like weeds.

This is done by using positive affirmations and declarations accompanied by deep emotions.

These techniques range from trauma release methods to Emotional freedom technique (also known as Tapping). You need to see an expert in these methods and see which one works best for you.

As a recovering people-pleaser, this was one that I really struggled with. I wanted people to like me and I did not like being criticised. As a result, when I was told to jump, my response was 'how high?' I also followed the rules set by authority figures and adhered to norms set by society without question.

When I made a decision, that I had enough, this had to change to. I had to break the expectations that others had of me. I had to put myself first and grow from there.

I would tell you; it was a scary experience but it was so worth it. My hands were trembling, my voice was shaking. There were times I wished that the earth would open and swallow me up because of the shame I felt.

Many mums have this canopy of shame hanging over their heads because of the expectations of others which have not been met. They run themselves ragged to please everyone to no avail.

Sometimes this is because of the need for validation or approval. It was almost as if we were hoping that someone would give us brownie points for getting things done.

Well, I have got news for you. There are no brownie points to be handed out but lots of criticism if you appear to fall short of the standard that some unknown or unqualified person has set.

The moment I realised that it was as though a piano of revelation fell on my head and questions started to unfold.

These are the questions that reset my thinking and helped my break free from the expectations of others:

a. What have I gained by conforming to the expectations of others?
b. What have I lost by conforming to the expectations of others?
c. What would happen if I stopped conforming to their expectations?
d. How would I feel if I did not have to conform to their expectations?
e. Who gave them the right to compel me to conform to their expectations? The answer to this last question is ME. I gave them the right and because I did, I can take it away when I choose. It always starts with a decision.

3. Breaking from the past

I remember when I watched the music video for `` Let it go from Disney's *Frozen*. I put it on repeat. I played it over and over again and when I got to the part where Elsa sang. *'The past is in the past, let it go, let it go...'* that hit my soul at a visceral level.

Many people have been held back by events in their past. They seem to replay that event over again and they can't seem to move forward. They are held by shame, guilt, fear and anger and that fuels the overwhelm that occurs.

It is the kryptonite that prevents us from soaring high.

I do not wish for you to develop amnesia but to detach your present self from the shadows of the past that have long gone.

When you start to tap into your superpowers, especially your power of intentional disruption, you start to discover who you are. That discovery uncovers your limitless potential.

For the sake of being unleashed, can you endure a moment of pain?

Can you endure the transient pain that is nothing compared to the pain you are going through as a result of overwhelm and exhaustion now?

You are doing this for you.

PRACTICE

1. What are the things that are holding me back?

2. What thoughts are constantly in my mind, making me make decisions that do not serve me?

CHAPTER 12- CREATING

I remember when I was younger, I heard the story of the glass cups which were filled with water up to the halfway mark. People were asked to describe the glass cup with water. While some described it as a glass half filled, others described it as a glass half empty. Generally it is said that the people who describe the glass as half-filled are more optimistic, and those who describe the glass as half empty, are more pessimistic. What they chose to focus on was reflected in their description.

Since we have covered the superpower of intentional disruption, I would like to bring some of that in this chapter.

What if we had a third description of the glass cup of water? My description is that of a glass that can be filled because it has a pitcher of water beside it. That is the concept of making things appear where they did not exist before. That is the POWER OF CREATING.

We all have this superpower and I would like to describe how it works. Before something comes into being, it needs to be created- once in the mind as a thought and then physically. That is the reason why the saying by Napoleon Hill, 'whatever the mind can conceive and believe, it can achieve,' rings true.

In the midst of chaos and overwhelm, it can be challenging to think about creating anything. The survival mind is triggered and the preoccupation is to fight, run or hide. That is; however, the best time to tap into this second superpower of creation.

We have immense potential to create anything including the future we desire. So start thinking about what you want and believe it can happen. Like Henry Ford said, 'If you believe you can or believe you can't, you are right.'

For you to be able to create anything, you need to believe that you can. This belief serves as the fertiliser for your thoughts. As you nourish this thought and take action you will see the physical manifestation.

In the account of creation, the physical manifestation of light, plants and animals came after the declaration for it to be. This shows us the power of words. We need to be mindful of the words we speak because words are powerful. Whenever we say something, it should be something that empowers and uplifts us.

When you wake up in the morning, tell the day what you want it to be. Tell the situation what you want it to turn out as. Do not sit down and cower hoping for things to change. If you create a desired goal in your mind but do not take action, it is merely a wish.

They do not change on their own, you need to take action. The realisation of your thought is in direct measure to the faith you have.

The Invictus poem written in 1875 by William Ernest Henley is an awesome piece of work that gets my entire being fired up in the midst of pain every time I read it..

Out of the night that covers me,

Black as the Pit from pole to pole,

I thank whatever gods may be

For my unconquerable soul.

In the fell clutch of circumstance

I have not winced nor cried aloud.

Under the bludgeonings of chance

My head is bloody, but unbowed.

Beyond this place of wrath and tears

Looms but the Horror of the shade,

And yet the menace of the years

Finds, and shall find, me unafraid.

It matters not how strait the gate,

How charged with punishments the scroll,

I am the master of my fate:

I am the captain of my soul.

The last two lines remind you of who you are and the creative abilities you have.

Start by setting an intention and make it compelling. I would give you an example. When I was holding my children as I laid underneath the duvet that winter morning, my intention was to stop this feeling of overwhelm and exhaustion that was crippling me and making me unable to do what I wanted to do, which in that moment was to play with my children.

I made this intention compelling by being very clear why that was important to me. My reasons were the two angels I held in my arms.

When I am faced with a challenging situation, here are some questions I ask myself:

1. What does this mean?

2. What else does this mean?

3. How can I use this?

As I write the answers in my journal, I do not rely on my mind to produce the thoughts and words but I recruit my spirit to BELIEVE and my soul to fuel my desire with the vibration of my emotions.

You can see how our entire being comes into play at times like this. One useful phrase that I use is 'Won't it be nice if something exceedingly great comes out of this?'

The ideas that follow from these reflections are then written and built up as plans. A good plan is time bound and chunked down. It almost appears like having a magnificent building made of LEGO pieces and you are able to isolate each piece that makes the whole. These pieces make taking action feasible and reduce the risk of overwhelm.

You need to be aware that you do not have to do all the tasks yourself. Remember the chapter on Taking stock of what you have? This is where you apply the human resources and systems who can do these things better, faster or more efficiently.

Delegate the appropriate tasks to them while communicating the deadline and any expectations you have.

Then, pick out 1-3 pieces you would like to work on and schedule them. Remember, creating is an intentional process too.

Like Stephen Covey said, 'The key is not to prioritize what is on your schedule, but to schedule your priorities.'

The process of getting these priorities completed while optimising your wellbeing involves breaking up your time.

I tend to use the Pomodoro. I set 25 mins slots followed by a 5 min break. After doing that 4 times, I take a longer break of 30-60 mins. In the breaks, do something that replenishes you. I will go into more details in the chapter on Nourishing.

At the end of each working slot, say to yourself, 'That was a great job, well done.'

You can then proceed to give yourself a high five, a hug or do a little dance into your break. Whenever you take breaks in between your session, your brain recharges, your body recharges, and you are able to do more and be more.

Creating starts from thought, recruits belief and requires action.

This superpower is one that makes the world go round and it is right inside of you. You are a SUPER MUM.

CHAPTER 13- BEING

I was watching a scene from *Kung Fu Panda* where Po was dealing with rejection from others who did not really like him at the Jade Palace. He was on the verge of quitting. As he stood underneath the peach tree, eating to deal with his emotions, Master Oogway, the elderly tortoise and senior master of the Jade Palace comes up to him. Some of the wise words he said was 'You are too concerned with what was and what would be.'

That is something that affects many of us. We dwell on the past and get depressed. We dwell on the future and get anxious.

I absolutely love this saying which I heard for the first time watching the cartoon.

'Yesterday is history. Tomorrow is a mystery. Today is a gift. That is why it is called PRESENT.'

The third superpower I would like to talk about is the POWER OF BEING.

This focuses on now and the continuous evolution in each moment. That is the essence of being.

When we put ourselves in the present moment, and enjoy the process, the risk of overwhelm is very low. Even the overwhelm that has accumulated, starts to dissipate.

Each aspect of our being- spirit, mind, soul and body can be given the gift of being. The ability to do that intentionally is a superpower.

Here are some ways by which each aspect is given this special gift.

SPIRIT

As mentioned in the earlier chapter, we are spiritual beings having a human experience. We are connected to God and each other. The state of being is a state of stillness and connectedness. When we feel overwhelmed, there is a disconnect in our spiritual essence. By rectifying that, calm, peace and harmony is restored.

This can be done by prayer which is simply communication between you and God. The most powerful prayer is the prayer of GRATITUDE. This brings about healing and restoration. It also opens you to an infinite source of wisdom, power and possibilities.

What a gift!

MIND

As we mentioned earlier, our mind produces thoughts automatically. They race by so quickly that we can hardly keep up. When we lose awareness of our thoughts, we get overwhelmed.

The practice of mindfulness increases our self-awareness and brings calm and harmony to our being. It also enhances our awareness of others thereby contributing to the distribution of peace and calm that we as mums can offer to our children and our loved ones.

I know what you might be thinking. 'I don't have the time to sit for long periods practising mindfulness.'

Don't worry about it.

There are many ways to practise mindfulness lasting a few minutes and they can be incorporated into your daily life easily.

1. Mindful breathing

This is one practice I do with my children for a couple minutes or even less. I use it when I end a task or before I begin a task. I use it when I get upset and need to reset quickly. It involves sitting in a comfortable position preferably in a quiet place (Mum Tip: the bathroom is a great place for us mums to do this).

- Take a couple of deep breaths in and out.
- Then pick a part of your body that is involved in the breathing process. It could be your nose, the back of your throat, your chest or abdomen.
- Taking a deep breath in slowly, notice what happens to that part you have picked. Are you feeling the cool breeze? Is it rising? Is it popping out?
- Pause and then breathe out slowly while noticing what you can feel on that part again. Is the air feeling warm? Does it fall? Is it going back in?
- Do this for 3- 5 times or longer if you want.

2. Mindfulness of thoughts

This is also another practice which involves you being in a comfortable posture.

- Take a couple of deep breaths. Then, breathing normally,
- Focus on your breath. As you breathe, you will notice different thoughts coming into your mind. Your aim is not to stop the thoughts but to notice them.

- For example, when a thought of worry comes to mind, say to yourself 'worry' and turn your attention to your breath. If another thought of your to-do list pops into your mind, say to yourself 'list' and turn your attention back to your breath.
- The aim is not to change what is but to notice and acknowledge the thoughts without judgement.

3. **Mindful listening**

In this practice, you are usually in a comfortable position.

- You don't have to be in a particularly quiet place but you need to be still.
- You can set a timer for a couple of mins or longer.
- Take a couple of deep breaths, close your eyes and listen.
- Take note of each sound you hear paying attention to the tone, pitch, frequency and intensity. You might even notice the synchronicity of the different sounds you hear.

4. **Mindful eating**

In this practice, you are eating but in a mindful way. Usually you want to remove electronics as they usually serve as distractions for this practice.

- Looking at the food, notice the colour, shape, and size.
- As you put in your mouth, notice the smell. Feel the texture. Pay attention to the flavours.
- As you chew, notice how the food moves in your mouth, mixes with saliva and gets grounded to a paste.

- Notice the process of swallowing.

This can be done for each mouthful.

- You can also think about the process of growing the plants.
- Think about the role each element (air, water, earth, fire) played.
- Reflect with gratitude on the work of the farmers, the truck drivers, the shopkeepers, who contributed time, energy and other resources to get the food to your plate.

5. **Mindful walking**

In this practice, you do not close your eyes or sit still.

- You are walking as usual but you are more aware of the movement of your feet, the swinging of your arms and the things around you.
- You notice them in the moment and acknowledge them without judgement.

SOUL

This is where we are present with our emotions and feelings. We can notice how we feel in each moment. It is the foundation of emotional intelligence. This can be expressed by writing in a journal.

Some people prefer using more creative ways of noticing and acknowledging their emotions using art, rocks, and other objects. Pick the one that suits you and enjoy the power of being.

BODY

We are so familiar with our bodies but we tend to be in a state of doing rather than a state of being.

To get our body in a state of being, you can use the practices described above or revisit the practice of body scan described in the chapter on taking note of the signs.

There is power in stillness. There is power in being.

By fostering these practices, we reflect who we are and evolve into who we are meant to be. You are a SUPER MUM.

CHAPTER 14- NOURISHING

How many of you have got plants? It could be houseplants or outdoor plants. Perhaps you have a farm, orchard or allotment.

The thing they have in common irrespective of their location is the need for nourishment. This is provided by the basic necessities- water, air, sun, nutrients from the earth.

The next superpower I would discuss is the POWER OF NOURISHING.

As mothers, we have the superpower of nourishing ourselves and others. However, we usually put others first and nourish them while we get depleted. This is a main cause of feeling overwhelmed and exhausted. The ability to nourish ourselves starts from the place of BEING and does not depend solely on what we do but on what we DO NOT do.

As in the previous chapters, I will describe nourishment in relation to each aspect of our being.

Remember though, that they are connected as we as human beings are.

The practices and benefits of the nourishment given to one aspect of our being flows to others.

SPIRIT

In the previous chapter, we talked about the role of prayer and gratitude. In addition, we should read spiritual texts which enlighten us. The knowledge acquired by reading and the practices of prayer and meditation open us up to receiving infinite wisdom from God, our source of infinite intelligence.

To nourish our spirits, we also need to do regular clearing out of activities which hinder our growth.

One of such activities is unforgiveness. This is an impediment to our prayer and connection to God. We will talk about this in more detail later.

MIND

The benefit of mindfulness cannot be overemphasized. In addition however, we need to feed our minds by reading, watching, and learning empowering information. This can be done using our five senses depending on our preference.

Journaling is a great tool for gathering, processing and expressing thoughts. It can serve as a foundation for the superpower of creating.

As with the spirit, we need to regularly declutter our minds of negative thoughts, words, ideas, beliefs and habits.

This can be done using mindfulness and affirmations.

SOUL

It is said that music is the food for the soul. I totally agree with that one. On those dreadful days when I laid there wishing it was a new day. And the nights I wished would come to end, I found solace in listening to music. The music opened my soul to express the emotions that were pent up in my state of overwhelm.

On some occasions, they got me moving to the beat, as my soul was filled with higher vibration emotions of joy, happiness and love.

As soulful creatures, we crave connection. The connection is not just with ourselves but with others. This connection is best when our mission, vision and purposes align.

As you connect with people who are in alignment with you, you need to remember to safeguard your space from emotional and mental energy that depletes you.

Do a relationship audit of people in your life.

For those who are detrimental to your wellbeing, you might need to remove their access to you. However, you do not need to shut everyone out, rather extend loving kindness while you are in a safe place.

Be mindful of the things you listen to, the information you consume on media, social media or even in conversations.

Create boundaries to safeguard your senses from being portals of negative energy.

BODY

I could write a whole book on the nourishment of the body.

In this chapter, I would explore it from the elements of nature and what I consider crucial to our wellbeing.

1. **Air**

We are alive because of our spirit and our breath. Without the breath of air, we die in minutes.

Breathing is an important part of nourishing our bodies. When we breathe in deeply, we not only make available more oxygen to our body organs, but we calm our minds.

2. Water

We are made up of more than 50% of water and our planet is also predominantly covered in water bodies. Without water we die in days.

Hydration is so important to our wellbeing. It is recommended that we drink 6-8 glasses of portable water daily. However there are multiple factors that can affect how much we drink.

Some of these factors include: your environment, your level of activity, the weather, your access to water, health conditions like heart disease, just to name a few.

Ensure regular hydration not just from water but from eating foods that are water-rich.

3. Food

Food is a basic necessity however; many people have shown that we can go without food for weeks if needed. Since we are talking about nourishment, we would refrain from extraneous circumstances.

Food can be obtained from plants or animals. People have different tastes and preferences. This is influenced by culture, experiences, and exposure.

Irrespective of your dietary preferences, the underlying theme in nourishment is making sure we are eating foods that agree with our bodies and eating in moderation.

4. Sunlight

This is that fireball that is thousands and thousands of miles away. It is the most important element providing the natural source of vitamin D which is an important hormone.

Vitamin D has been linked to our physical, mental and emotional wellbeing. Ensuring we are adequately exposed to early morning sunlight even for a few minutes daily is beneficial.

Also depending on your skin type, be mindful of burning if you are prone to.

5. Grounding

This is when they are connected to the earth. It is such a useful practice that has been found to improve physical, mental and emotional wellbeing. In some spiritual texts, it is reported how people felt the need to connect to Earth when they required spiritual guidance.

6. Movement

This can take many forms and is not restricted to joining a gym. This is not another book about exercise.

As a mum, I know how busy we can get and going to the gym can feel like a chore. So you can take 5 mins, 10 mins or even 20 mins to ensure movement. There are some fun activities that you can do even with your children.

Some include: dancing, nature walks, running, swimming, playing catch.

There are some exercise snacks which I do in between my tasks lasting 1-2 mins.

They include: jumping jacks, burpees, and sumo squats,

which are really good for strengthening our bones as women.

These movements not only provide strength and flexibility to our bodies, but they can be a way to build our relationships, improve our mood and enhance our mental wellbeing.

Practising Yoga, Pilates and other forms of movement are very useful to enhance your wellbeing. Pick the one that suits you. Be flexible with what movement you would like to engage in at every given moment. Most importantly, make it fun.

7. **Rest**

The value of taking breaks in the form of rest and even sleep is massive.

Taking regular breaks from tasks as discussed in the previous chapter is so beneficial for your wellbeing and productivity. Ensuring that you are having good quality and quantity of sleep is also very important. Pay attention to what your body is saying and take a break.

Like we mentioned in the nourishment of the other aspects of our being, we need to declutter when it comes to our bodies.

This can take the form of what we eat and drink, items we use that are toxic to our bodies, or clearing our physical space just to name a few.

Nourishing is a superpower and we need to make the choice to put ourselves first. We are SUPER MUMS.

CHAPTER 15- GROWING

When I was in primary school, we had a project to study the growth of a bean seed. We were to place it in a clear container, water and expose it to sunlight daily. Each day we were to record any changes. I noticed the seed appeared to separate in the middle initially. Then the roots and shoot appeared.

As the days went by, the roots spread and the shoot got longer. Eventually, it gave off leaves and pods which had bean seeds inside.

We are like that seed. Every day there is a new change in the different aspects of our being. As we continue to adequately nourish ourselves, we grow to become a better version of ourselves and become productive.

As mums, we have produced the beautiful angels we call children and they are seeds themselves. They, however, are still connected to us and benefit as we continue to grow.

The SUPERPOWER OF GROWING is an innate ability that we need to consciously cultivate. That is why it is said, "When you stop growing you start dying." - William S. Burroughs

Sometimes we need to be stimulated to grow. One of the most common stimuli is adversity. This can come as the threat of loss or loss itself. It can be a single blow or multiple hits.

My stimuli of growth were the loss of my father, the loss of my wellbeing and the loss of my identity. They were painful experiences which I would not wish on anyone but without them,

I will not have the increased spiritual awareness, mental wellness, emotional resilience and physical stamina I am experiencing now and developing daily.

What has your stimuli for growth been in the last week, month and year? This is a question we need to ask ourselves frequently. It is a good way to reset and reflect on our growth.

We do not need to wait for adversity however we should embrace it when it comes. In the face of increased stress leading to overwhelm, we can use the situation to enhance our overall wellbeing.

This is the evolution from being to BECOMING.

Do not compare yourself with anyone but who you were yesterday. This removes the possibility of low vibration energy like jealousy and envy.

Growing helps you to appreciate who you are. Yesterday was the 2.0 version of you. Tomorrow, the 3.0 version is updating. How intriguing is that!

The growing process involves the use of other superpowers to help it manifest such as the superpower of disrupting, creating, being and nourishing.

Like I did in primary school with the bean plant, I find it very useful to monitor my growth. I am able to do this by journaling. Journaling should be a daily practice that should be reviewed regularly.

It helps to ask yourself questions that provoke introspection and reflection. This makes us more intentional with our actions. It helps us utilise our superpowers more efficiently. It guides us on the path to avoid the kryptonite that weaken our ability to be who we truly are and become who we are meant to be.

I have found very useful the use of plain sheets in a book but soon discover one of the best journals I have ever seen aimed at your growth.

This journal has plain sheets for you to record your thoughts electronically. However, at those times when you are having writers' block and you are staring at the blank sheet, it prompts you to write by asking you thought provoking questions. How awesome is that!

I highly recommend the Growthday journal which can be accessed **HERE**.

Growing daily is the best gift you can give yourself and the way to evolve from who you are to who you are meant to be.

This superpower leads us to our purpose and explores our infinite potential.

Utilise it daily because YOU ARE A SUPER MUM.

CHAPTER 16- GIVING

'The secret to living is giving.' - Tony Robbins

While growing up, my parents were so generous- giving their time, energy and resources. I noticed how they not only gave to my siblings and me but to others as well.

Even in challenging times, my father would give to people in need. Some people exploited that but he was so kind-hearted and gave freely anyway.

Despite working as a civil servant, putting all his children through private school education, we never lacked. I remember seeing the great joy in his eyes when he was giving. He truly lived and was celebrated even in death.

When we look at nature, we see that giving is happening around us. The plants give us oxygen. We give off carbon dioxide which the plants use. The Earth gives us plants for food. The animals that eat it give their poo as manure that nourishes the plants. And the cycle of life goes on.

When you give, you let go of what you are holding on to and make room to receive more. I also found that it is when it seems hardest to give that we should give cheerfully.

There is a parable of a poor widow who was making an offering with others on a Sabbath day. As the wealthy people dropped bags of money into the treasury box, this lady put in two small coins. While watching, Jesus said something very interesting, yet powerful.

'The woman had given more than the rest.' Why? you may ask. This woman gave all that she had while the others gave from their surplus. This was a lesson for me not to wait until I have more than enough to give. That realisation has been a blessing.

This is the SUPERPOWER OF GIVING

As mums, we are always giving. This can be connected to the hormone Oxytocin which promotes bonding.

The superpower of giving is especially activated when we give without expecting anything in return.

It has been found that when you give, there is an interplay of chemicals in the brain namely Serotonin, Dopamine and Oxytocin. This gives an elevation in our mood. We find out that we experience a greater sense of calm and happiness.

Hence in a state of emotional overwhelm, giving can serve as an antidote. It moves your mindset from a place of scarcity to a place of abundance. When we give, we tap into our knowledge, and belief in the abundance that abounds.

Giving is not confined to material wealth or physical things. It comes in different forms. Offering help to someone in need such as seen in volunteering goes a long way.

You can give compliments, a smile, a warm hug, a kind word, your time, your energy, your presence.

Another way you can give is to give others the opportunity to help you. This is something we mums struggle with. We give to everyone but do not allow others to give to us.

I struggled with receiving from others for a very long time but with a reframe of my thinking, I was able to tackle that. The reframe I did was to say, I am allowing others to give to me because I want to give them the opportunity to experience the joy that comes from giving.

That changed my outlook and gave me grace to give and receive graciously.

This superpower blesses not only you, but others around you. It takes us to a place of upliftment of body, soul, mind, and spirit.

CHAPTER 17- FORGIVING- A GIFT TO YOU

Forgiveness is a gift you give yourself. It is not something you should withhold; otherwise you would be punishing yourself.

Being fearful for so long really drained my energy. After a while, I started to feel angry at myself, then to those who hurt me. That anger made me create a vault around myself. 'No one can hurt me now,' I thought.

However, I was hurting myself because I was angry with myself. After all, I was the one who gave them the power to hurt me.

There are times when we experience painful situations and we say things to ourselves like 'I should have known better; I was so stupid: Should have seen it coming or even 'what did I expect?'

These are mean things that we would not say to anyone who confides in us that they are going through a similar ordeal. So why do we say that to ourselves?

Could it be unreasonable expectations that have been set for us and we decided to 10X it?

The anger we feel changes to shame, blame and guilt and we find ourselves at low energy vibrations. That is why we feel drained and overwhelmed.

The remedy to this lies within us. That is the SUPERPOWER OF FORGIVING.

You will offend yourself many times and many people will offend you.

Forgiving is not letting yourself or them off the hook. It is recognising what was done, releasing the negative emotions linked to it and growing from it.

Did I hear you say it is easier said than done? I can totally relate. It took me a while of cyclical forgiving and unforgiving especially when dealing with a repeat offender.

However, when I recognised that I am going to live with me for the rest of my life I was committed to make this work. There is no place to run and no place to hide.

Besides I did not like the headache, body pain and backache I was feeling. That is when I knew that I needed to get this sorted.

I read lots of books, researched and prayed hard. One of my favourite books was *'Letting Go'*. This helped with the expression of my emotions rather than the suppression and repression that was the culturally acceptable thing to do.

But my liberation came with the mirror work described by one of my coaches. This broke me down and helped me build myself back up, joining the pieces together with precious metal and love.

I add a new layer every day.

The mirror work is a daily practice of you looking into a mirror and saying a few sentences.

The first set is 'I am proud of you for...' (list 7 things that you are proud that you have or that you have done)

The second set is 'I forgive you for...' (list another 7 things that you forgive yourself for doing or not doing)

The third set is,' I commit to you that... ' (list 7 things that you are committing to do for yourself henceforth)

As I say these statements in front of the mirror, I look straight into my eyes, say my first name before each statement and hug myself all through.

Hugging myself was a personal statement I was making by my actions, which said 'You are seen. You are heard. You are held. You are loved.

The first few days had me having ugly cry scenes. Tears on my cheeks, snort down my nose, eyes red and swollen. At the end of each session, I looked like I was beaten up.

As I progressed, the frequency of these ugly cry scenes decreased. I felt seen, heard, held and loved.

I love myself so much. My relationship with me has deepened and is still growing. I was able to release shame, anger and guilt in relation to my vulnerable moments when I felt powerless.

I still do my mirror work and some repressed memories come up every now and again. The gift of forgiving yourself is so priceless

CHAPTER 18- FORGIVING OTHERS

How could they do that? That was so mean. What did I ever do to them?

I was angry that I had allowed people to treat me so badly. Initially I thought that if I did what they wanted, they would be happy and I would not be criticised. How wrong I was.

That anger became resentment. Having these thoughts made my blood boil.

Though anger had served as fuel for me, now it was acid.

I had even started to skip saying 'Forgive us our trespasses as we forgive those who trespass against us' in the Lord's Prayer.

How sad is that!

That was the pathetic place I found myself.

'Why was it so hard?' I thought.

And then I came across this phrase, 'Forgiving is not letting someone off the hook. Forgiving is a practice you do to heal yourself because you are worth it.' As I wrote that phrase in my journal, I started the journey towards forgiving and letting go

This chapter covers the SUPERPOWER OF FORGIVING by extending it to others.

In the last chapter we talked about forgiving yourself. It is easier to forgive when the other person is aware and repentant.

But what if the other person is either unaware or unrepentant? What do you do then?

Hold them in resentment? Oh no!

The popular quote ' Unforgiveness is like drinking poison and waiting for the other person to die.' rings true.

It has been found that there are changes in your body when you harbour feelings of anger, resentment or unforgiveness. These could cause headaches, raised blood pressure, hormone imbalance and other features of stress.

Hence, it is critical to forgive and let go for your own good. I used multiple practices and tools to help with the process and I still use them till today because I am worth it.

Most of these practices require repetition. They could take a min or longer.

Here are a few tools that I use:

1. **Ho'oponopono practice**

This Hawaiian practice uses a short yet powerful set of sentences. It is used to set things right. The words said are:

I love you.

I am sorry.

Please forgive me.

Thank you.

These words can be repeated several times. You can have the person present or do it in their absence.

2. Well-wishing practice

This practice takes between 2-5 mins. It can be adapted to meet your needs. I use it to send warm wishes to my loved ones, friends, those who have hurt me and those I do not know.

I use the acronym WASH.

For each group, I say

May (name of person or people) ... be well,

May (name of person or people)... be at peace.

May (name of person or people)... be safe

May(name of person or people) ... be happy

If you are angry with someone, you may speak through clenched teeth initially (I did that) and after a while, as you let go, it flows better

3. Emotional Freedom Technique (aka Tapping)

This technique popularised by Nick Ortner, founder of The Tapping Solution is such a useful tool for a diverse number of conditions and situations. It focuses on tapping gently on the acupuncture pressure points while making statements to release tension and calm the nervous system.

This process takes a little longer than the ones listed above but the relief felt is immediate and refreshing. I used the tapping meditation **'I refuse to forgive'** and the result was remarkable.

This can be accessed online or on the tapping solution app.

The lower energy levels that come with anger, resentment and unforgiveness cause emotional drain. Forgiveness moves you from a place of overwhelm and exhaustion to a place of hope and higher energy vibrations.

The idea of sharing these practices and tools with you is to express to you how you can tap into your power of forgiving to heal yourself holistically.

CHAPTER 19- CONNECTING

"When mind, body, and spirit are in harmony, happiness is the natural result." - Deepak Chopra

That is the essence of CONNECTING. It shows that we are better when all aspects of our being are in harmony. We are also better when we as humans are in harmony. I absolutely love this superpower because it is so amazing.

Imagine you want to bake a cake. And despite your efforts at mixing the flour, sugar, and eggs in the bowl they remain separate. How would the cake be made?

To get the desired outcome, the ingredients would need to be mixed together.

As mentioned in previous chapters. We are not just made of body. We are made of soul, spirit, mind and body. When we are able to effectively connect each aspect of our being, we would enjoy holistic well-being.

If, however, we forget, ignore or neglect one aspect of our being, it leads to ill-health, stress, overwhelm and feeling exhausted. That's not what we want. The spiritual should be able to communicate with the physical. The emotional should be able to communicate with the physical, and vice versa.

When all aspects of our being are connected in harmony, your power of creating is magnified.

People talk about manifesting. Manifesting is not just wishing for something to happen. It is knowing deep within our being, that our body, soul, mind, and spirit, are all in alignment with what we desire. And it comes to be.

By being connected within yourself, you bring into physical form, things that were initially in the first phase of creation- the thought phase.

Can you imagine what it would be like if this could be done at will?

Or, if you can recreate the future you desire and deserve?

This is an area I am exploring and so far it is looking great.

Apart from being connected within ourselves, let's talk about being connected with each other people.

I really love this definition of connection by Brené Brown.

"I define connection as the energy that exists between people when they feel seen, heard, and valued; when they can give and receive without judgment; and when they derive sustenance and strength from the relationship." — Brené Brown

As mums, we are the super glue in the family. We tend to be the peacemakers among our children. When there is a quarrel or fight, they come to us to settle the matter. Based on different parenting styles, we desire to smooth things over.

We initiate friendships with other parents in the early years of our children's lives and foster childhood bonds. We arrange and facilitate play dates. We are the ones who organise the social events at our children's schools, in our neighbourhood, at work and in our communities.

So you see, we are super connectors utilising our superpower of connecting.

We also show our children the social skills that enable them to be great connectors too. They learn this by observing the way we connect to ourselves, and others.

'But how can we use this superpower when we are feeling overwhelmed and exhausted? I hear you ask.

That is the best part. We need to draw on our knowledge that we are not alone.

We start feeling overwhelmed and exhausted when we feel isolated. Or even when we feel that our situation is so unique and no one else has experienced it. We need to tap into the collective resources that our connectedness brings.

This comes in the form of asking for help.

It is not a sign of weakness when you say, HELP!

It is a sign of strength.

We have been conditioned to think that we should know all the answers and know how to do everything or else we are useless. That is not true. Each person has got their awesome superpowers which contribute to the abundance in the world.

We have people who have experienced what you are going through and can serve as a guide such as a mentor.

Our community can serve as support and even a source of strength. A community that experiences discord and disconnection, will end up in chaos, war and strife. However, if the community has connecting superpowers actively manifested. It enjoys prosperity, growth and productivity.

I am drawn to share the biblical story of the tower of Babel. This was when a group of people were so connected and they agreed to build a tower reaching up to heaven. God recognised this and said, 'Behold, the people is one, and they have all one language; and this they begin to do: and now nothing will be restrained from them, which they have imagined to do.' (Genesis 11:6 KJV). That is the power of connection in a community.

We also have experts. These could come in the form of health care professionals, mental health experts, financial experts, legal professionals and coaches.

As a clinician, I would always advise people to seek professional personalised help. There are times when you require medication, counselling or some form of therapy to deal with feeling overwhelmed and exhausted.

So regularly ask yourself the following questions to evaluate your superpower of connecting.

1. How am I connecting all aspects of my being- spirit, mind, soul and body?

2. How is my connection with others?

3. How can we rectify the disconnection that exists among us?

This superpower of connecting is what helps us to grow. It is the vital element of a community.

Let's find our common ground and work to uplift each other.

I would like to share this story about a farmer who was very unwell and he thought he was dying. He had 12 children who did not get along. He was very worried that when he died, his family would be in chaos. He was not sure what to do, but then asked each one to go out to the farm and bring a stick.

As they gathered around his bed, they started arguing about who had the best stick. Feeling quite frustrated, he asked them to give him the sticks. He gathered the 12 sticks and held them together with a twine.

He then gave the bundle of sticks to his first child and asked him to try to break them. He tried, but failed to break the bundle of sticks. The farmer then asked each child to have a go at breaking the bundle.

However, none of the children was able to break the bundle. He then took the bundle untied the sticks and asked each one to take his stick. They all did. He then asked then to break their sticks. With minimal effort, each one was able to break his stick. By doing this, he was able to demonstrate to them that they are stronger together.

Taking a cue from this, we are meant to connect with each other. We are meant to collaborate rather than compete. Together we stand, divided we fall.

CHAPTER 20- HARNESSING THE SUPERPOWERS

A muscle that is not used atrophy. A skill that is not used is lost. A power that is not used diminishes. That is why we need to harness our superpowers. This is done by consistent practice, taking action, and using the power.

The more you use the power, the greater it grows.

I remember watching 'Matilda', an amazing movie about a little girl who had special abilities which were not appreciated by her family.

She unintentionally discovered that she had the ability to move objects with her mind. As time went on, she was practising how to use her ability so that she could help her teacher and classmates. As she practised, her power grew. She was able to move multiple objects and control electronics from a distance.

That movie reminds me that we have superpowers. Sometimes we don't recognise them. Other times we are reluctant to use them or even forget to use them.

By using them consistently, every single day, probably multiple times during the day, we will magnify those powers and even uncover more. While we have listed some superpowers we have in the previous chapters, there are still many to be uncovered. And I'm so intrigued because I know that you will uncover your superpowers.

In this chapter, I am going to share with you some practices that I put in place to ensure that I am harnessing my superpowers. To ensure this, I try to make them easy to do and habitual.

As you probably would have gathered by now I love reading books, and watching movies too.

There is a book, *'Tiny Habits'* by BJ Fogg which describes a simple model to make a behaviour into a habit.

There were four main elements of behaviour change.

Behaviour change (B) happens when motivation (M), ability (A) and a prompt (P) converge at the same time. That is the Fogg model, B = MAP.

Motivation can be provided by positive or negative influences. Positive influences include a positive peer group or a desire for a pleasurable outcome. Negative influences include moving away from pain or negative experiences.

The second element that needs to be present is the ability to perform the behaviour. Everyone has the ability to be who they want to be. However, we need to believe that we can.

So far in this book we have spoken about the important role that belief plays in the attainment of any goal. Your belief in your ability is directly proportional to the achievement of that behaviour.

Thirdly, we need prompts to make the behaviour take place. Prompts act as stimuli. They wake you up to who you are and what you are supposed to do.

We sometimes require stimulation to get things done. These could be internal or external stimuli.

When you have a prompt, the belief in your ability to achieve something, and motivation, whether positive or negative, you are most likely to change your behaviour.

As an example to demonstrate this model, I will focus on the superpower of nourishing. Remember, all these superpowers are in continuous tense, because they require continued action.

A lady who had been struggling with eating right and exercising goes to the doctor for a routine check. Her blood test revealed that she has pre-diabetes. She is told about the risk of developing diabetes. She also recalls how her dad needed to have a below knee amputation due to complications of diabetes. She is terrified and wants to change. As a result she is given support to have lifestyle changes.

In this scenario, the desired behaviour is about proper nourishing of her body.

Motivation comes from the desire not to develop diabetes and the desire to change when she thought about her dad's complication.

Ability is related to her belief she can change, as well her willingness to take action

Prompt was the blood test result suggesting she had pre-diabetes.

For her to achieve her outcome, she would need to chunk the desired behaviour into multiple steps.

For example using the B= MAP model,

Behaviour- Lose 5kg in 2 weeks

Motivation- A reward for taking action

Ability- She is able to go for walks before work

Prompt- Her walking shoe placed beside her bed.

What is that behaviour you would like to incorporate into your life?

Take some time to make it easy to do, get motivation to do it and prepare a reward for when it is done.

There are many ways to incorporate these healthy habits into your life but I would share a few ways.

- Be creative with what works for you, your situation and your lifestyle.
- Remember, we are all made up of spirit, mind, soul and body.
- So as you select your choice activities, let them nourish your entire being.

My spiritual practice when I wake up in the morning is that of gratitude, and prayer. What I tend to do is use music to express it. As I sing or hum, the melody uplifts my soul, as I show gratitude with my spirit. I usually put in a couple of dance steps which exercise my body. So you see how you can use one activity to take care of every aspect of your being.

It is crucial to have a morning practice. However, you need to incorporate self-care practices all through the day. 'How do you do that?' you might ask.

That is done by using your superpower of disrupting to break up your time. As you break up time to do your tasks, break out time to do your self-care.

There are self-care activities that you can do, in two minutes, five minutes, 10 minutes and 30 minutes. Select the one that suits you and schedule it.

A Pomodoro is a useful tool to facilitate that.

As you do that, ensure that you have a prompt for example the ding of the timer. Also, have mini rewards or celebrations when each step in done.

That builds your motivation muscle. When you do these things repeatedly, they become automatic and habitual requiring less energy.

You have got this SUPER MUM.

CHAPTER 21- COMMON PITFALLS

Have you watched the scene on television where your favourite hero defeated the villain and had the opportunity to hurt the villain but chose not to? Usually this is followed by the hero walking away and then the villain attacking him.

In some cases, the villain uses an object that weakens the hero. Like in Superman, the object is KRYPTONITE.

We all have the kryptonite that hinders us from being our best selves. Recognising and getting rid of these kryptonites is critical to our growth. As supermums, we can also be impacted by kryptonite.

So far we have talked about all the amazing superpowers we have. Our superpowers are not limited to what is in this book. We will continue to discover them as we go along.

However, there are times when we turned our backs and the kryptonite come close or get connected to us. That is usually when we get into a state of overwhelm and feel exhausted.

That is when we forget who we are and what we are capable of.

Here are a few kryptonites we need to be mindful of:

1. Limiting yourself

The first kryptonite is usually self-inflicted and I think it is the most important.

Henry Ford said, 'If you believe you can or believe you can't, you're right.' I totally agree with that statement. Belief in yourself, your abilities, and God are the key to achieving anything. The moment your belief starts to dwindle, you cannot inspire faith in others.

Here are a few questions you can ask yourself when you are faced with the kryptonite of limiting yourself.

a. When I have this feeling of being limited, how does it make me feel?

b. Is there a way I would like to feel if I am truly unlimited?

c. What would it be like and feel like if I could get rid of this limitation?

2. Listening to naysayers.

We are always going to have opposition, as we navigate through life. Sometimes these naysayers actually feel that they are doing us a whole lot of good. They can be your family and close friends.

When you tell them your audacious goal, they tell you reasons why you should not go after it. And you know that they are doing it out of concern for you. It becomes apparent to you that they do not understand your vision.

In this scenario, you should understand that it is okay for them not to understand your vision. Keep showing love and respect as you do not impose your vision on them.

Sometimes the naysayers are people that are plain nasty e.g. trolls on social media. They give criticism without considering what adverse effect it has.These people might not even know you.

They may have limited information about you and feel the need to judge you.

There are also others who you might have had a misunderstanding or an altercation with, and they just want to get back at you.Perhaps an unrepentant enemy.Those are the people who are potentially kryptonite. However, there are ways by which you can deal with this type of kryptonite.

Sometimes you can have a discussion with them.

Ask question like, 'How can we resolve this issue amicably?' or What would be a good common ground for us to co-exist amicably?

Setting boundaries is an effective strategy and will not only safeguard your mental wellbeing but your emotional wellbeing.

Here is a guide to setting healthy boundaries. You can adapt it to meet your specific situation or needs.

Step 1- Identify your boundary

This is when you define in clear terms to yourself what your non- negotiable is. Because we have different standards, our set of values may defer. There are some things that we can tolerate and some that we cannot.

Become clear about which ones you would not tolerate and set your boundary to include them.

Step 2- Understand why you need this boundary

You need to know why this boundary is important to you. It would guide you in those situations when you need to be firm. It also safe guards you from repeatedly experiencing a distasteful event.

It serves as the back bone to your decision to care for you.

Step 3- Decide on the consequence if the boundary is breached

This is what happens to the relationship or person is they violate or do not respect the boundary you have set. This decision is done in advance .It helps you to keep your word to yourself. Remember the quote by Maya Angelou "When someone shows you who they are, believe them the first time."

Step 4- Communicate directly

This is a very important step. This is when you communicate your non-negotiable to others. This eliminates the possibility of ignorance.

Step 5- Do not apologise for your boundaries

This goes without saying. Do not be sorry for loving yourself. Do not apologise for placing your wellbeing first.

Step 6- Address boundary breaches when they occur

Be clear in your communication when you boundary is breaches and what the implication of violation would be.

Step 7- Trust your gut

This is that sixth sense we spoke about earlier. Pay attention to what it is telling you and take action.

3. Not stopping to smell the roses.

As mums we do so many things and are constantly in motion. As a result we move so quickly through life. We do not take time to stop, listen, relax or take a breath. We are constantly moving.

We are not human doings we are human beings. We need to practice being present in the moment.

The way to tackle this kryptonite is practising mindfulness.

You can be mindful in everything. You can walk mindfully. You can clean your home mindfully. You can cook mindfully. You can eat mindfully; you can listen mindfully. The list is endless.

These are ways by which we can build that muscle of intentionality. The intention of stopping to smell the roses, the intention to have breaks to recharge.

Here are a few checkpoint questions we can ask ourselves:

a. When was the last time I took a look around me?

b. When was the last time I took a break to appreciate the beauty of my current situation.

c. When was the last time I spent time with my loved ones, just having fun and being a child again.

If the answer to any of these questions is a duration longer than you are comfortable with, stop what you are doing and smell the roses.

4. **Not staying consistent with small movements.**

Have you heard the story about the tortoise and the hare?

In this story, the tortoise and the hare were having a race. As the race started, the hare ran quickly while the tortoise moved slowly. At a point the hare looked back and could not see the tortoise in the distance. So he decided to take a rest because he was sure to win. When he woke up however, he saw that the tortoise was crossing the finish line and no matter how fast he ran he could not win that race.

Take small persistent action is better than large inconsistent leaps.

Moral of the story- Keep moving even if you are moving slowly.

So take consistent action on those habits, discussed in the previous chapter. Incorporate them into your daily life.

5. **Keeping the wrong crowd around you.**

This kryptonite includes the people, media and energy we surround ourselves with. It requires a certain level of situational and environmental awareness.

Someone might serve as a limitation when they negatively affect our focus and growth. Being selective about who you allow in your space can been helpful.

When we interact with media or social media be intentional about the impact we desire to have on it and vice versa. For that reason, I do not go on social media first thing in the morning. I also refrain from binge watching the news.

You can walk into a room and there is so much negative energy that it drains you.

Being aware of the energy you bring to a space and the energy contained in the space you enter will help you to make a choice that is beneficial to you.

a. Are the people around you aligned with your purpose?

b. Is the media you are consuming elevating your spirit, body, soul and mind?

c. Do you feel uplifted by the energy around you?

This kryptonite could weaken you and prevent you from taking action and moving ahead.

6. Staying isolated, not asking for help.

Sometimes people have this notion that a supermum is someone who does not ask for help but does everything flawlessly.

That is not what makes you super. You are Supermum because of the superpowers you possess within you.

The moment you start to think that you are the only one going through adversity, you multiply your pain. As a result, you need to be aware of this kryptonite, and take charge.

Many times as mums we ignore the messages our body is whispering to us or just put up with it. Sometimes we do not want to be judged and as such do not ask for help.

Society has labelled women who spoke up the past as being hysterical and they promote the image of us being quiet and sitting still. We need to recognise that sitting still and not asking for help is not helping us.

So ask for help and be prepared to receive help.

Offer help and be prepared to receive recognition for the help you have rendered.

Let's place collaboration above competition. Let's grow together.

Let's empower each other as the Super mums that we are.

CONCLUSION

The superpowers described in the book point toward our holistic wellbeing. Imagine wht the world would be like if every mum knew that she has these superpowers and she can use them at will.

She also knows that even on those days when she is exhausted, or feeling overwhelmed, that she is a SUPERMUM.

Even on those days she feels she made a mistake. She is still a SUPERMUM. When society is criticising and shrouding her in shame, she is a SUPERMUM.

She feels empowered by the knowledge of having the superpowers of disrupting, creating, being, nourishing, growing, giving, forgiving, connecting and even more that are yet to be uncovered.

She is not a SUPERMUM because of what she does but because of WHO SHE REALLY IS and the superpowers she possesses with.

This is a message to all the mums out there:

EVERY MUM IS A SUPERMUM!

ABOUT THE AUTHOR

Dr. 'Dunni is a life & wellbeing coach, family doctor, international speaker, teacher, author, entrepreneur and mum who empowers mums to eliminate the feeling of overwhelm and exhaustion by tapping into the super powers within. This is to ensure the continued enhancement of their overall wellbeing so they can live the life of calm and abundance they desire and deserve.

Her journey into health and wellbeing started when she decided to be a medical doctor over two decades ago. She is a practising family doctor and educator of future medical doctors.

Her personal development and exploration into holistic wellbeing practices and lifestyle medicine started after the death of her father.

She practises a holistic view of health and wellbeing and encourages others to do the same.

She is proficient at using natural, scientific and medical wellbeing concepts to explain in simple terms practical ways and strategies to avoid ill health and promote overall wellbeing in body, mind, soul and spirit.

This is made available by provision of online courses, written, video and audio online content, books, coaching and regular events such as challenges, where wellbeing strategies and tactics are shared to enhance holistic wellbeing on a daily basis.

You can learn more at https://www.drdunni.com

Printed in Great Britain
by Amazon

76439149R00078